The Drama of Gender

Wor(l)ds of Change
Latin American and Iberian Literature

Kathleen March
General Editor

Vol. 38

PETER LANG
New York • Washington, D.C./Baltimore • Boston • Bern
Frankfurt am Main • Berlin • Brussels • Vienna • Oxford

Yolanda Flores

The Drama of Gender

Feminist Theater by Women of the Americas

PETER LANG
New York • Washington, D.C./Baltimore • Boston • Bern
Frankfurt am Main • Berlin • Brussels • Vienna • Oxford

Library of Congress Cataloging-in-Publication Data

Flores, Yolanda.
The drama of gender: feminist theater
by women of the Americas / Yolanda Flores.
p. cm. — (Wor(l)ds of change: Latin American and Iberian literature; vol. 38)
Includes bibliographical references and index.
1. Latin American drama—Women authors—History and criticism. 2. American drama—Hispanic American authors—History and criticism. 3. American drama—Women authors—History and criticism. 4. Feminism in literature. 5. Women in literature. 6. Latin American drama—20th century—History and criticism. 7. American drama—20th century—History and criticism.
PQ7082.D7F65   862—dc21   99-26923
ISBN 0-8204-3958-4
ISSN 1072-334X

Die Deutsche Bibliothek-CIP-Einheitsaufnahme

Flores, Yolanda:
The drama of gender: feminist theater
by women of the Americas / Yolanda Flores.
−New York; Washington, D.C./Baltimore; Boston; Bern;
Frankfurt am Main; Berlin; Brussels; Vienna; Oxford: Lang.
(Wor(l)ds of change: Vol. 38)
ISBN 0-8204-3958-4

The paper in this book meets the guidelines for permanence and durability
of the Committee on Production Guidelines for Book Longevity
of the Council of Library Resources.

© 2000 Peter Lang Publishing, Inc., New York

All rights reserved.
Reprint or reproduction, even partially, in all forms such as microfilm,
xerography, microfiche, microcard, and offset strictly prohibited.

Printed in the United States of America

Dedication

Por su inspiración, a mi abuela Aurora H. Soto
y a la memoria de mi abuelo José Soto.

En agradecimiento por el amor y apoyo que me han
brindado, a mi madre Micaela Flores y a la
memoria de mi padre Simón E. Flores.

For being there for me, to my siblings Irma, Gustavo,
Carlos, Armando and Arturo.

ACKNOWLEDGEMENTS

It is a happy occasion to have a space to record my gratitude to the people and institutions that helped make this book exist. The love of my family and the intellectual companionship of my friends and colleagues in Bakersfield, Berkeley, Chicago, Ithaca, and other parts of the globe sustain me personally and professionally. I am particularly grateful to Connie Graham, Jura Oliveira, Yvonne Singh, Susan Gilmore, Margo Perkins, Annette Passapera, Eliza Proença Pereira, Lorna Marlow, Enid Pérez, Anne Rubenstein, Irene Daniel, Kat Avila, Mary Chavez, Ashley LaJune, Sylvia López, Christine Virgen, and Theresa Hebert.

At Cornell University, I am thankful to Debra Castillo, Thomas Holloway, and John W. Kronik for the encouragement and guidance they offered to me while this study was still in its embryonic stage. Special heartfelt thanks to John W. Kronik for his embrace of this project and support in my professional career. I can only hope that I will be honoring my gratitude by emulating John's professionalism. As an undergraduate, I was lucky to have been trained by hispanic feminists whose scholarship and passion in the classroom has been a source of inspiration: Emilie Bergmann, Gwen Kirkpatrick, and Francine Masiello. I am especially grateful to Emilie Bergmann for her continued support throughout my career: I am deeply moved by her professional generosity. At the University of Chicago, I wish to thank George Haley and Martha Schaffer. Without a doubt, I owe my intellectual development to this group of formidable teachers and scholars.

In Brazil, the faculty of the Programa de Integração da América Latina at the Universidade de São Paulo generously allowed me to participate in and benefit from their program. My stay in Brazil was crucial to the development of some of the ideas on which this study is predicated. For their helpfulness, I also wish to thank the librarians at the Museu Lasar Segall. ¡Muito Obrigada!

The playwrights Leilah Assunção, Josefina López, and Susana Torres Molina kindly gave me access to some of their unpublished texts and to personal interviews. For this and for trusting me with their work, I am grateful to them.

I also wish to thank the institutions that financially supported my research. Thanks to an anonymous donor at Cornell University, I was able to secure a fellowship, which made a six-month research stay in

Brazil possible. Cornell's Graduate Student Travel Grant sponsored a second research trip to South America. Research in Mexico City was partially funded by a Chapman University Faculty Summer Research Grant, and a Faculty Grant-in-aid rendered the technical support. At Chapman, I am thankful to Vice Provost Barbara Mulch for her support of my work.

Emilie Bergmann and Irene Daniel read the entire manuscript and provided helpful and constructive comments. The Brazilian Chapter, in particular, benefited by the critical reading by Margo Milleret, Jura Oliveira, and Eliza Proença Pereira. Ismael "Smiley" Calderón assisted with technical support.

At the University of Vermont, I thank the Department of Romance Languages and Literatures for their enthusiastic reception of my work. Their support is a source of encouragement for the future undertaking of projects of this magnitude.

I wish to acknowledge permissions to reprint the following copyrighted material: excerpts from Leilah Assunção's *Lua nua*, (São Paulo: Edicões Símbolo, 1993), Carmen Boullosa's *Cocinar hombres,* (Puebla: Universidad Autónoma de Puebla), 1987, and Josefina Lopez's *Simply Maria or the American Dream*, (Houston: Arte Público Press), 1992.

Last but not least, I thank Heidi Burns, Senior Acquisitions Editor at Peter Lang, and Kathleen March, Series Editor, for their interest in and support of this study. I thank them and the staff at Peter Lang for their patience in working with me.

This book is dedicated to the members of my family because without them, I would not be who I am. I owe them my sense of work ethic, of human decency, and my thirst for justice. As I argue in this book, the personal invariably colors the creative, intellectual, and professional worlds. ¡Mil gracias a todos!

Errors of interpretation, fact, and omission are all my own.

TABLE OF CONTENTS

Introduction: Staging Dramatic Feminisms	1
Chapter 1: Dirt and Domesticity: Constructions of "Race" and Gender in Contemporary Brazilian Theater	21
Chapter 2: (De)naturalizing Desire: Homoeroticism and Performance	41
Chapter 3: On Dramatic Bodies, Witches and Feminine Dramaturgy	57
Chapter 4: Staging Difference: Performing Border Identities	73
Conclusion	95
Endnotes	99
Bibliography	107
Index	127

Introduction: Staging Dramatic Feminisms

Staging the North American Critical Context[1]

The field that interfaces women playwrights, theater, and feminisms has only recently become the object of critical and, to a lesser extent, pedagogical attention. The special contribution of this book is to fill a scholarly gap existing in the juncture between women's dramaturgy and feminisms as they manifest themselves on contemporary stages across the American continent. With the rubric "Americas" I wish to highlight the many linguistic, cultural, and political layers comprising each country that falls under such a heading. This study will make no attempt to examine all of the continent and will concentrate on Brazil, Mexico, Argentina, and Chicanas from the United States. This book seeks to address questions of gender and genre, as it situates the plays under consideration within their specific context and in dialogue with feminist dramatic theories. A contextual approach embedded in a materialist methodology allows me to underscore how issues of race and class are dramatized on stages across the Americas.

One of the main objectives of North American and English feminist literary criticism is to rescue from obscurity texts written by women. By disseminating the work of women writers, feminist critics question the validity of a literary canon that accounts for only one view of the world—men's. The criteria by which works are measured and judgments are made to determine whether a work is worthy of being studied are components of the feminist defiance of phallocentrism. A second important task for feminist critics is to study female characters in male-authored texts with the tacit assumption that they carry the author's desires and fantasies of what women are and ought to be: to uncover the possible works of a misogynist ideology is essential to a feminist project (Munich 250). These two goals of the feminist literary agenda remain important tasks for literary critics, especially for those who work with literature or genres considered marginal from the traditional North American and European perspectives. In regards to genre, feminist critics have struggled to broaden its definition by including forms of writing historically ignored by the canon, like women's diaries and women's journalism. Plays written by Latin American women writers, for example, comprise an area of Hispanic literature that has not been thoroughly studied in North American universities, a fertile source for further historical investigation and critical attention.[2] The basic concepts on which this study is grounded bear clarification. I take "man" and "woman" to designate biological conditions; "feminine" and "masculine" are socially constructed definitions aimed at governing biological concepts (Stimpson 174).

In *Femininity*, Susan Brownmiller reveals how the fabricated notion of femininity has coerced women's lives, for this concept is a set of rules that dictate the way women should look, dress, and behave. In their desire to achieve the image of the ideal woman, as prescribed by the social conventions of the day, many women have participated, perhaps unknowingly, as conservative agents of these dictums (3-14). Yet, today some feminists are more willing to question these rules overtly: for example, Chicana playwright Josefina López deals with the problem of making fat a feminist issue. In *Real Women Have Curves*, she presents a feminist character who, unlike the other female characters in the play, refuses to submit to the pursuit of the ideal woman's body as dictated by the fashion and model industry of New York and Los Angeles. A feminist theory that especially pertains to the discussion of women and theatre is Judith Butler's "gender act theory," whose proposition extends beyond the divisions of a gender system based on biological categories. Grounding her approach on an epistemological framework, Butler claims that gender subjectivity is in no way a stable identity or locus of agency from which various acts proceed; rather, it is an identity tenuously constituted in time—an identity instituted through a stylized repetition of acts. Further, gender is instituted through the stylization of the body and, hence, must be understood as the mundane way in which bodily gestures, movements, and enactment of various kinds constitute the illusion of an abiding gendered self. (270)

If, in fact, gender is constituted by the performance of acts, what is the difference between this type of acting and the one that takes place in a theatrical representation? From a feminist perspective, what are the advantages and disadvantages of connecting this theory to the representation of a dramatic text? Is this theory predicated on the idea that all subjectivities are constructed equally: does it account for cultural and ethnic variations in the construction of subjectivities? How do women playwrights experiment with the construction of gender, either "feminine" or "masculine"? What can a feminist critic make of, for example, Mexican playwright Sabina Berman's piece *El suplicio del placer*, in which two characters who in their looks and behavior are not easily identifiable as either "feminine" or "masculine" play out typical gender struggles for power as they continuously exchange a semiotically "masculine" signifier—a moustache? Or of the play . . . *Y a otra cosa mariposa*, by Argentine Susana Torres Molina, who introduces on stage five female characters who dress as men in front of the audience and perform male characters quintessential for their low regard of women? Just as at the beginning of the play, these characters dress to perform male characters, at the end of the play they take off their masculine costume to return to their "feminine" dress. What do these gender "acts" have to do with the "performances of power"? What do these questions reveal about the nature of theatre and of the "theatrical quality of life"? Should this system based on "acting" and "performing" be called into question? How can questions of truth, justice, and equality be advanced in a social system implicitly founded on a notion of falsehood? If femininity and gender categories are nothing more than performative social acts, what, then, do individuals with female or male sexual organs have in common, and what do these organs indicate?

Is there such a thing as the "écriture féminine" advanced by theorists like Hélène Cixous and Luisa Valenzuela? Do authors believe their writing is determined by their sex? These questions have been widely discussed by feminist critics, theorists, and writers, but there is no universal answer among these groups nor within the constituencies of each group. I tend to agree with Butler's "gender act theory," which is predicated on ideas advanced by Simone de Beauvoir in her 1949 classic feminist manifesto, *The Second Sex*, in which she challenged previously held universal postulations that demarcated gender categories according to biology and called attention to the social construction of gender identities. Butler's theory carries de Beauvoir's ideas further as she argues that gender identities are cultural constructs in need of repetitive "performances" to insure their distinction. So, when a woman dramatist like Griselda Gambaro asserts that playwriting "is the most masculine form of writing" ("Interview" 193), I take this statement to refer to cultural impositions that conditioned women to adopt a passive, non-aggressive role.

In regards to the variations among feminist literary criticism and theories, I concur with Robyn Warhol and Diane Price Herndl that it proves more constructive to "present various feminisms, a significant number of voices and approaches functioning alongside other feminisms . . ." (xiii). Just as there is no universal "woman" subject, neither is there a single feminism. Yet, the framework of constructing a false universal woman is necessary because it allows the different feminists and feminisms to reach the consensus that women have been misrepresented in, when not completely excluded from, literatures, histories, and other forms of cultural productions, and to recognize that, with all their differences and particular goals, women need to build coalitions among the groups of feminists in order to be more effective in bringing about social change.

The publication of Kate Millet's *Sexual Politics* marked 1970 as a key year for feminist literary criticism. However, the first study to link feminism to the analysis of dramatic texts was not published until 1988: Sue-Ellen Case's *Feminism and Theatre*.[3] After its publication, this book was subjected to telling criticism by theater scholars who called attention to its historical inaccuracies.[4] One important omission noted by Ellen Gainor is that, by locating the practice of feminism and theater within the emergence of academic feminist literary studies in the 1970s and thereafter, *Feminism and Theatre* fails to acknowledge earlier theatrical feminist practices, for example, the North American suffragist plays of the 1930s and 1940s. Gainor's observation points to the danger of concentrating one's scholarship exclusively on academic trends, which sometimes do not coincide with practices outside of the academy.[5] Her critique evokes the limitations of critical methodologies, that by not crossing disciplinary boundaries, run the risk of producing spare or erroneous postulations. Notwithstanding its limitations, *Feminism and Theatre* is useful for charting in a systematic way some of the most salient versions of feminisms pertinent to the study of women and theater: radical, materialist, and women-of-color. In addition, this study brought attention to women playwrights from various literary traditions, for example, the mid-tenth-century German nun Hrotsvit von Gandersheim and Aphra Behn in seventeenth-century England. Case also discusses the work of the first woman playwright of the Americas, the seventeenth-century Mexican nun Sor Juana Inés de la Cruz.

It may be useful to set forth the basic currents of the field of feminism and theater:

1) Radical women's theater is founded on radical feminism, which underscores women's culture as essentially different and separate from the patriarchal culture of men. Lesbian feminism and theater are situated within this framework, for they are based on women's identification with other women. The radical feminist lesbian position assumes that her primary relationships are with other women; the heterosexual woman is differentiated because, privileging her

relationships with men, she is presumably male-identified. According to this way of thinking, heterosexuality separates women from one another by making women define themselves through men and compete among themselves for the privilege that comes through men and their social standing (Case 62-77). A problem with this definition is that it does not yield space for the existence of woman-identified heterosexual women, that is, women who choose men as their sexual and life companions but whose point of reference is still woman-centered.

2) From a materialist feminist perspective, women's experience cannot be understood outside of their specific historical context, which includes a particular type of organization and unique developments in national history and political structure. The function class plays in social arrangements means there are crucial differences between upper-middle-class women and working-class women (*Feminism* 82-83). In instances where the role that class plays in women's experience and in the production of literature and criticism is highlighted, one discovers that, for the most part, critics in the United States continue to privilege the study of upper-middle-class women. When the cultural productions of working-class women are given critical attention, their class background is often effaced. The tendency to privilege upper-middle-class women's literature is partly due to the reality that the institution of criticism and the academy as a whole, like other professional fields, from their inception to our days, have been predominantly reserved for the socially and economically privileged—first men and now women. So even as working-class individuals entered the profession, they have been slow to bring issues of social differences into academic discussions. However, this is an area in which change, as small as it may be, has recently begun to take effect. Examples are the critical attention given to working-class literature by academics like Paul Lauter and Cora Kaplan and the editorial efforts of Warhol and Herndl, who designate a section of their *Feminisms* anthology to class-centered analysis. With respect to the academy's upper-middle-class constituency, it is salubrious to witness Carolyn Law's and C. L. Barney Dew's effort to compile a collection of essays by or about working-class academics.[6] Among the possible topics they suggest are the theoretical and political issues involved in moving from the working class to professions in higher education and pedagogical concerns for educators from the working class (376). Just as women's experience is marked by a patriarchal society, so too in a capitalist society are working-class individuals affected by their standing in this system. A materialist approach permits space to examine how

social organizations affect the production of culture and criticism; it makes visible the invisible "performances of power" behind these operations.

3) Feminist studies that focus on women of color fuse aspects of both materialist and radical feminism. Class is a central issue to women of color, since their ethnic communities are most often bound by both color and class. As Case notes, "the understanding of the hierarchical nature of classes under capitalism is essential. When ethnic identity is used to relegate people of colour to the role of surplus value in the labour force, race becomes identical with class in the market place" (Feminism 97). The American context of the term "women of color" is an important factor because it was white women's lack of sensitivity to ethnic oppression that prompted Blacks, Chicanas, and other nonwhite women to challenge the presumed homogeneity of the North American feminist movement in the late 1970s (Feminism 96). "Women of color," thus, is a political term created to build coalitions among American women who bear the triple burden of gender, race, and class oppression within a capitalist North American society. It is essential to contextualize this term in order to avoid grouping women from third world countries into this category or incorporating American women of color with third world women and feminisms without establishing their differences.

A representative example of this problem is Chandra Mohanty's anthology *Third World Women and the Politics of Feminism*, where she tries to define the category of "third-world women": "Third world is defined through geographical location as well as particular socio-historical conjunctions. It thus incorporates so-called minority peoples of color in the U. S. A." (2). While using the term "women of color" interchangeably with "third-world women," Mohanty advances that the term "women of color"

> . . . designates a political constituency, not a biological or even a sociological one . . . What seems to constitute "women of color" and "third world women" as a viable oppositional alliance is a common context of struggle rather than color or racial identifications. Similarly, it is third world women's oppositional political relation to sexist, racist, and imperialist structures and systems that determines our potential political alliances—[a] "common context of struggle." (7)

Chicana critic Katheryn Rios notes the contradictions and problems inherent in the use of these terms as categories of analysis:

> How can an alliance of "women of color" not be based on "color or racial identifications" but, rather, a "common context of struggle"? What is that common struggle then based on? Isn't it not only their opposition to "sexist, racist, and imperialist structures," but the fact that they are subjects of those "sexist, racist, and imperialist structures" by virtue of their color (as well as class and gender) that unites women of color in a common struggle? And how can "women of color" and "third world women" be used as equivalent terms? This would mean that a fourth-generation Chicana in the U. S. would be considered a third world woman as much as a Mexicana, a woman born and living in Mexico; or a woman born and living in non-industrialized Guatemala; is she not a "woman of color"? (1-2)

In her study *"There are no Chicanas in Maquiladoras: Difference and Identity in Context"* Rios examines the material conditions that affect identity and self-naming in a group of "third-world women"—Mexican nationals who work in maquiladora industries in border towns between the United States and Mexico—and a group of North American "women of color"—Chicanas. It would seem that, aside from geographical locations—that is, the Mexican nationals' daily crossing of the border to their jobs in the United States—the differences between these two groups are minor, but that is not the case. While Chicanas may be concentrated in the lowest paying jobs in the United States labor force, they do have certain advantages in comparison with the Mexican maquiladora worker. Legal status in this country, language, and more "Americanized" social behavior are determinant markers of difference which allow the working-class Chicanas more job options than their Mexican counterparts. Not only do Chicanas have a wider range of alternatives, but these jobs tend to offer better health and safety protection than those available to the Mexican. These border town Mexican nationals view themselves as distinct from individuals of Mexican ancestry born and raised in the United States; they acknowledge common ancestry with Mexican Americans or Chicanas but feel that differences in language, values, and behavior render them dissimilar. Some Mexicans pity the Chicanas for being neither Mexican nor American (Segura 65).

Another important distinction that should be noted is that for the same reasons that Chicanas, in a global context, are not third-world women, neither are they Latin American women. Again, one must recognize the flawed results that stem from grouping Chicanas in anthologies, conferences, and course syllabi of Latin American women without acknowledging the North American background of the Chicanas' experience. The significant differences between Latin American and Chicana writers are observed by Mexican writer Elena Poniatowska:

> Con las chicanas, el problema también es la clase. La escritora mexicana no viene de las clases trabajadoras ni tiene una relación de inmediatez con el campo y la fábrica que sí tienen las chicanas . . . Sin proponérselo, de manera muy explícita vencieron los prejuicios de clase, los raciales, y la descriminación social y económica de que eran objeto, hasta llegar a sus propios sentimientos de baja estima. (3)

Relative to Mexican maquiladora women, Chicanas enjoy certain privileges derived from their first-world birthplace. When Mexican and Chicana writers are compared, working-class Chicanas (all Chicanas that I have studied are of working-class background) are at a disproportionate social and economic disadvantage. Similarly, in her "testimonio," *"Puerto Rican Writers in the U.S., Puerto Rican Writers in Puerto Rico: A Separation beyond Language,"* Nuyorican writer Nicholasa Mohr candidly speaks of how she feels a sense of camaraderie more with other American writers who ultimately share the same goals than with Puerto Rican writers from the island. African-American writers Alice Walker and Ishmael Reed, Raymond Carver's and Tillie Olsen and Chicana Denise Chavez are writers with whom Mohr finds more affinity than with the Spanish-speaking Puerto Ricans from the island. In a Latin American context, Chicanas and Nuyoricans are the equivalent of the socially, economically, and politically marginalized poor, indigenous, black, mulatto, and mestizo women that inhabit, to various degrees, all Latin American countries: Guatemalan Indian Rigoberta Menchú, Bolivian mine worker Domitila Barrios, and Brazilian favelada Carolina Maria de Jesus are Latin American women comparable, but not equal in social standing, to Chicanas in American society. It is worth noting that these Latin American women chose to tell their "testimonios" with the specific objective of denouncing conditions that they desire to change. Their writing is inseparable from the discrimination they experience in their societies, as is the case of most Chicana authors.

Yet, unlike Chicana and Nuyorican who have had sufficient interpretative power to allow them to be the sole producers of their literary and artistic creations, the work of Menchú, de Jesus, and Barrios has been realized only through the mediation of a second person who does not belong to the same racial and economic group as they do. With tenacity and courage some women of color struggle to attain interpretative power. Helena María Viramontes affirms that when she enrolled in a creative writing Master's program, her professors repeatedly told her that her work did not meet the "accepted" standards. Viramontes finally abandoned her graduate program when one of her professors said to her that she should write about "people and not about Chicanos."[7] Another writer of color, Amerasian playwright Velina Hasu Houston, had a similar experience when she was told by a professor in graduate school that she would never become a real playwright unless she began to write for a wider audience. The fan in the office diminished the quality of the sound and left Houston uncertain, she reports, whether the professor said *"wider"* or *"whiter"* (2). Elena Poniatowska's honest perception reveals that Chicanas are subjected to an institutional racism absent in the upper social spheres to which the majority of the most successful Latin American women writers belong. To the racism she experienced in the academy, Viramontes responded by fighting back against the system that had downgraded her work; she did not give up writing. Instead, she has continuously struggled to publish powerful stories about Chicanos and other more recent immigrants, victims of the same sort of racism that Chicanos have long experienced. For Chicana writers like López, Viramontes, and Moraga, the feminist adage "the personal is the political" is not empty rhetoric; it is the dictum that regulates their daily lives and creativity. It is important to clarify, of course, that not all incorporations of Chicano literature into Latin American projects are inherently problematic. When differences are made explicit, such undertakings can serve comparative purposes and trace the cultural ties between these two groups.[8] Furthermore, these enterprises can provide a space in which Latin Americanists are introduced to the study of the cultural artifacts created by North American Latinos. The *Latin American Theatre Review, Gestos,* and the conferences organized by the academic institutions in which these journals are auspiced yield a forum for publications and lectures on Chicano theatre. Yet, Chicano theatre remains Chicano theater; it does not become Latin American theater. Just as Chicano signals a North American context, so does the term women of color. Shange, Houston, Moraga, and López, among others, are U.S. playwrights of color who have articulated the inability to separate the politics of living from one's ethnocultural identity and gender.

Significantly, theater critics have been at the forefront in acknowledging the relationship between their work and their own subject position. Among this group, Elin Diamond, bell hooks, and Yvonne

Singh have published articles in which they theorize about the relationship between their subject as it interfaces with their critical work. For example, Diamond, who is white, admits:

> When I, a white critic, approach the plays of Adrienne Kennedy, a black artist, am I not interpellating her texts with my models, making her and them something ideologically comfortable to deal with? (131-32)

Diamond and hooks engage in a mode of criticism which is personally and theoretically self-reflexive, a critical practice which disrupts false dichotomies personal/political, intellectual/experimental, theory/practice (Singh 194). In her study *"Staging in the Funnyhouse: The Dramaturgy of Adrianne Kennedy,"* Singh notes a fact that seems obvious to someone engaged in the production of theatrical performances but that often escapes critics who approach drama solely from a literary perspective: the very nature of the theatrical representation begs for the disruption of critical paradigms applied to other genres. In the theatrical performance racial identity and ethnicity have a visual quality, and voice has an aurality communicated through performance (194). While the visual dimension afforded by the theatrical representation is absent in critical reading and writing, these issues are not prevented from influencing a critic's project, methodologies, and her/his own subject position. Breaking the boundaries between subject/object, this study acknowledges that it is written from the perspective of a critic who is also a woman of color.

Latin American Women Playwrights:
Historical and Theoretical Postulations

The colonization by the Spanish and Portuguese marked the lives of Latin America's women in peculiar fashion.[9] In the case of Spain, I am referring to the Spanish preoccupation with "limpieza de sangre," that is, to the Renaissance obsession with proving that one was "pure" of Jewish or Moorish blood. This mentality transposed to the indigenous Americas fomented racially hierarchical, stratified societies. The more European-white, the higher the social standing. While it was common for white men to have illegitimate children with the indigenous and black population, white women were responsible for maintaining the purity of the race. Consequently, white women were discouraged, if not prohibited, from mingling in domains outside of their homes; their space was the domestic sphere in which they were trained to be good mothers for the future leaders of their societies (Martin 2-8). Jean Franco notes that

> ... the division of the traditional city into public [male] spaces and private space where women's power derives from motherhood and virginity has deeply affected both political life in Latin America and the imaginary repertoire on which literature draws ... women characters [are allegorized] in their virtually invariant position of mother, prostitute or love object. ("Self-Destructing" 105)

Historical evidence reveals that nonwhite women moved more freely in public spheres—nondomestic space—than their white counterparts. This freedom often translated into the marketplace of prostitution: prostitutes in literature are monotonously nonwhite women of low social standing. But important counterevidence shows, for example, that having fewer restrictions than white women was an enabling factor that inspired the participation of lower-class "soldaderas" in the Mexican Revolution. Whether they knew it or not, their presence was a public political act. Besides, it is worth remembering that male writers of the "corridos" have converted tough female combatants into submissive, romantic figures like "la Adelita" and have characterized well-known soldiers and other women who did not fit customary roles as nonfeminine, manly, and exceptional (Deutsch 263). Needless to say, the darker indigenous, black, mestizo, and mulatto women had no access even to the most elementary way of attaining literacy.

For reasons discussed above, white Latin American women, those with open avenues to literature, have been relegated more strictly to the domestic/private arena than their European and North American counterparts. The remarks of the nineteenth-century Brazilian playwright, Maria Angélica Ribeiro, attest to this difference:

> A mulher brasileira, se não quer sujeitar-se ao escárnio dos espirituosos e ás censuras mordazes dos sensatos, não tem licença para cultivar o seu espírito fora das raias da música ao piano e das de algumas frases, mais ou menos estropeadas de línguas extrangeiras! ... As européias, sim, essas inteligentes e talentosas, podem estudar e escrever; poetar ou compor dramas e romances; podem satisfazer as ambições de sua alma, ter culto e conquistar renome ... Entre nós,

não, que nada disso se pode dar! O que sai de lavra feminina, ou não presta, ou é trabalho de homem. (27)

The reality of Ribeiro's observations, the constraints imposed on women's creativity, is supported by the fact that during her lifetime only one of her plays was published—*Os Cancros Socias* (1866). Written twenty years before Brazil's abolition of slavery, this play discloses antislavery sentiments similar to those manifested in Gertrudis Gómez de Avellaneda's novel *Sab* (1841). As with Ribero, the Cuban writer's creative inclinations were discouraged; at an early age her intellectual interests earned her nicknames such as "la atea" and "la doctora." These two authors, like Sor Juana Inés de la Cruz centuries earlier, give evidence of what some critics of contemporary Latin American women writers describe as a distinctively feminine concern for the marginalized from the vantage point of the dominant society and culture (Castillo 57-61).

With all the privileges attached to upper-class status, white race, and access to education, Latin American women writers from Sor Juana to Elena Poniatowska, in various degrees and forms, have confronted restrictions imposed by their machista societies. However, a question not always raised is how these women, marginalized from patriarchal centers of power, use their interpretative leverage to construct race, to represent those who because of their racial make-up are even more at the periphery.

Many feminist literary critics have utilized the model of public/male space in opposition to the private/feminine domestic sphere as paradigms to explicate the social predicament of women's lives and the specificities of feminine writing. Latin America's history exhibits the conditions that propagated this dichotomy and suggests its effect on women's intellectual and nondomestic development. The earliest and most common traditional space from which women's writing has emerged is the domestic space of the home reflected, in genres that are more private, such as women's diaries. Unlike prose and poetry, drama is the arena most removed from the confines of domesticity: theater is overtly public. The woman who ventures to be heard in this space takes greater risks than the woman poet or novelist; nonetheless, it may also offer her greater potential for affecting social change.

In *Making a Spectacle*, Lynn Hart writes: "the women playwright's voice reaches a community of spectators in a public space that has historically been regarded as a highly subversive, politicized environment" (2). The potential for upsetting the social status quo resides in the genre's ability to function as an image of the world and a generator of new images. For example, in the Hispanic literary tradition one can recall Lope de Vega's *"Arte nuevo de hacer comedias,"* in which he prescribes the rules to be followed by other dramatists, prescriptions that are intrinsically connected to the audience's reception of images generated in the theatrical representation. The hierarchical order of Spanish Renaissance society was maintained and reflected in the comedias: aristocratic literary verses were reserved for characters belonging to the nobility; lower-class servants behaved according to the script demanded of individuals of their social standing. Characters' behavior that did not correspond to the class ranking they represented signified a direct attack on society's harmony.[10] The public nature of playwriting is a factor that explains why historically women have been timid to practice this form of artistic expression—especially so within the Latin American context because writing plays is culturally the most "masculine" of literary activities. Griselda Gambaro states:

> . . . it demands a different sort of aggressiveness . . . Theatre and Cinema are connected with society, with the social situation . . . theatre demands a confrontation with the audience; it demands that you connect with other people . . . I believe that all acts of writing are impudent, shameless, but drama especially, because one knows that one is going to be on stage through the actors . . . That's why theatre is much more aggressive, it shows more and whatever it shows. It is immodest. ("Interview" 193)

While there is evidence that attests to the public/private opposition, the uncritical use of this division can lead to the failure to recognize important changes in twentieth-century Latin America. I am referring to a critical practice that relegates women and their writing to domesticity without taking into account Latin American women's involvement in and contribution to the public feminist political agendas.

The collaborative effort of the contributors to *Women, Culture and Politics in Latin America*, edited by the Seminar on Feminism and Culture in Latin America, has produced an extraordinarily knowledgeable study that challenges the notion of women's exclusive seclusion in the domestic sphere.[11] These scholars note that 1910-1950 was a crucial period for the advancement of Latin American feminist organizations: during these years major cities witnessed the emergence of the first generation of urban, literate women, many of whom chose the profession of schoolteachers. These "maestras" were important figures because they constituted the largest percentage of the Latin American women involved in Pan-American feminist political organizations and conferences. The goal of these organizations was to reform the inadequacies of the traditional forums from which women were allowed to speak and act. Together these women searched for strategies that would relieve them of the burden of patriarchal tradition and fulfill their need for social reform (Bergmann 2-6). Out of a context of more accessible education and literacy emerged two prominent women of letters: Gabriela Mistral and Alfonsina Storni. Mistral, a schoolteacher by formation and the only Latin American woman to receive a Nobel Prize in literature, has been canonized as a poet particularly concerned with religious fervor, children, and motherhood. Biographers and editors of anthologies, mostly male, have often highlighted these themes as a way to justify the fact that Mistral did not marry and have children; they have failed to pay attention to writings that reveal another dimension of hers: poetry that intimates an individual concerned with world political affairs. For example, Mistral wrote the poem *"Campeón finlandés"* to celebrate Finland's resistance to two Russian invasions during World War II. In a similar fashion, Alfonsina Storni has been commonly regarded as a talented but troubled poet who in a romantic fashion committed suicide. Storni's poetic themes do refer to events that reflect her biographical reality. Yet, the Argentine poet's journalism and her involvement in political activism that sought to change the social status of women has been generally overlooked. Gwen Kirkpatrick, in her essay, *"The Journalism of Alfonsina Storni: A New Approach to Women's History in Argentina,"* challenges old conceptions of *Storni* by bringing to light feminist activism. As the contributors to *Women, Culture and Politics* observe, traditional images of women encompassing everyday life, domestic activity, religious practices, marriage, and the body reinforce a male elitism that claims serious intellectual, artistic, and political work as the exclusive preserve of men (vii).

    Latin Americanist feminist scholars, it seems to me, stand to benefit from historical investigation; literary critics can recover works, writers, genres that do not fit the male model of women's lives and that problematize sexual boundaries.[12] Besides, much male-dominated political decision-making is done in private, exclusive spaces. Alain Rouquié notes in *The Military and the State in Latin America:*

> Behind the "public stage" of popular sovereignty there is a "private stage" based on relations of domination. Every attempt at participation that is not controlled, that is not the result of an agreement of the participants on the "private stage," is therefore seen as a threat to the pact of domination ... (34)

The uncritical application of the public/private paradigms to this century's realities may silence historical evidence that disrupts this assumption and perpetuates the omission of women's work in nontraditional subversive enterprises.

In her study, *Theatre of Crisis: Drama and Politics in Latin America,* Taylor observes that North American and European dramatic criticism of the 1960s, the '70s, and to a lesser degree the '80s, contributed to the devalorization of Latin American theater. The critical training of academics in this period tended to decontextualize plays by focusing on universal themes and recognizable theatrical models and traditions. In the name of objectivity, critics frequently covered the text with a critical discourse that buried the emergent dramatist's voice (14). Powerful defining groups outside Latin America claimed that, judged by accepted standards of artistic excellence, the theatrical activity of these countries was "underdeveloped." I borrow the example cited by Taylor to prove a point: In 1968 the editor of Drama Review summarized a theater research trip taken by two prominent contributors to this journal. One of these critics stated that Latin American theater deserved the attention of our society because, "though it has problems and is a little backward—[it] can be approached and understood in the same ways as United States and European theatre" (qtd. in Taylor 15). Taylor correctly observes two implicit problems in these comments: 1) Latin American theater has to meet "our terms"; 2) the designation "backward" subverts the implied acceptance of this theater. The other critic was left with the following impression: "In Latin America there is no theatre . . .There are some dead shapes moving about on proscenium stages . . ." (qtd. in Taylor 15). The final words of the editor of Drama Review's special issue on Latin American theater were that this theater uses recognizable dramatic forms, but he concluded that they were "clumsily borrowed" (first world writers are influenced, third world writers borrow) and that this theater "savors too much of a humble effort to please" (qtd. in Taylor 15). Only by decontextualizing Latin American plays could these scholars find meaning in them in terms of Western background and experience; only by deterritorializing the works could they justify the plays' existence. Given the remarks of these critics and the prestige of the Drama Review in theater and academic circles, who would feel compelled to read these plays? Who would want to invest time and energy researching the theatrical activity of this area? Who would want to teach this field? Criticism, as Edward Said has perceived, can play an important, though unacknowledged, political role in marginalizing literary productions (25).

The examples discussed earlier demonstrate how hegemony (the ideology of the dominant first world critics in this case) passes as objective criticism, for it depends on privileging certain models that then exclude other cultural manifestations. Arif Dirlik in *"Culturalism as Hegemonic Ideology and Liberating Practice"* suggests that this exercise denies contemporary relevance to the culture of the other (24). The colonialist attitude disclosed by these critics' evaluation of Latin American theater is not limited to the rating of this genre; to various degrees, there is a tendency among some North American scholars to downgrade Latin American cultural products. Juan Villegas observes: "the plurality of Latin America's many realities is typically reduced in the name of universality. On a subtle level, Latin America's many differences and idiosyncrasies simply failed to interest those who looked for Western equivalents" (58).

Latin America and the Americas. Throughout this book the term "Latin America" has designated the twenty-five nations south of the Rio Grande River—countries that have a common history of colonization, turbulent independence, racial conflicts, machismo, and a shaky sense of self-definition and identity (Taylor 222). But each country is distinct from the others; each displays its own national sentiments. Uruguayan writer Ida Vitale observes:

> Se habla de realidad latinoamericana, y en realidad tal unidad es relativa. Lo que es verdad para un mexicano, no lo es para un uruguayo. No hay una norma genérica. Y viceversa . . . Y diría que algunos países latinoamericanos de valores, de fronteras adentro, son tan nacionales como los europeos . . . (223)

While Simón Bolívar's dream of a unified Latin America was cherished by some of his nineteenth-century contemporaries, the reality of the twentieth century is that Latin Americans see themselves as entities different from one another, and, generally speaking, they do not think of themselves as Latin Americans. They "become" Latin Americans when they travel or live abroad to differentiate themselves from Europeans or North Americans (Taylor 36).

This discussion has focussed on staging the historical, critical, and theoretical foundations for the study of dramatic texts by women from various countries of the American continent. I call these dramatists "women of the Americas" not with the intention of making them into a homogenous group but precisely to acknowledge differences. Like the term "Latin America," "Americas" is a construct, a fabrication that suggests diverse realities experienced on this continent. How many layers of "Americas" are in what is called Latin America? How many ethnic and cultural variations of Americans are there in the United States? Which culture of "Latin America" are we talking about when we discuss Latin American writers and thinkers? This study seeks to call attention to the limitations inherent in all-encompassing, general categories by highlighting the many layers of cultural and racial variations exiting in the Americas.

The Woman of Color as Spectator and Critic

> The theatrical quality of life, taken for granted by nearly everyone, seems to be experienced more concretely by those who feel themselves at the margin of events either because they have adopted the role of spectator or because, though present, they have not been offered a part or have not learnt it sufficiently well to enable them to join the actors—those who do not participate in a social system are less likely to see it as natural and are therefore more sensitive to its contrived or constructed quality.
> (Burns 11)

As Burns suggests, those who have historically been on the margins are more sensitive to the fabricated basis of society and culture. The artificial construction of these concepts is now being contested by members of groups that have not been given the opportunity to participate equally and fully in society. Gender, 'race,' and class are determinant factors that have contributed to the invisibility of particular groups. For some members of a North American ethnic minority who find themselves as "marginal actors" in this dramatic reality, their presence, even their very survival in academia, signifies an opportunity to further the efforts to democratize the production and interpretations of knowledge.

This book traces the diverse feminisms staged on theaters across the Americas. The plays examined—*Lua nua* by Leilah Assunção (Brazil, 1987), *Simply María or the Amreican Deam,* by Josefina López (U.S. Latina, 1988), . . . *Y a otra cosa mariposa,* by Susana Torres Molina (Argentina, 1981), and *Cocinar hombres* by Carmen Boullosa (Mexico, 1987)—all exhibit a desire to deconstruct patriarchal notions of gendered roles and behaviors, of compulsory heterosexuality, and of dramatic forms. This demystifying enterprise is accompanied by the aim to create a variety of identities, more true and just to the reality of women's lives. The divergent historical and political contexts from which the plays emerge influence the way in which the authors express their feminist vision.

In the first chapter, I examine a realist play, *Lua nua*, where the source of conflict centers on the plight of a middle-class, professional, white woman negotiating the boundaries between the public and private sphere, a "dupla jornada de trabalho" that impinges upon her. This play raises the issues that nowadays confront women who, in obtaining access to the professional world, benefited from the early feminist movements. The discussion further contextualizes the difficulties, such as motherhood and domestic responsibilities, that continue to affect the productivity of women playwrights, whereas, generally, male authors are not confronted with these obstacles. Furthermore, *Lua nua's* treatment of the institution of domestic service raises complex questions about simple feminist notions of "woman" as a homogenous category united by common oppression. Materialist feminism maintains that women's experience cannot be understood outside of their specific historical, political, and national structure. From the perspective of the employer, one can apprehend the play as espousing a feminist position, but the presence of the domestic servant calls attention to the limitations of this type of feminism. Although *Lua nua* is a realist play, a dramatic form viewed by some feminist dramatic theorists and critics as reactionary and contradictory to feminist goals, the play nonetheless, still represents, from a feminist perspective, issues affecting the daily lives of middle-class women and the racially marked and disempowered working-class women. Hence, realist drama is not necessarily inconsistent with feminist aims.

An Argentine case study constitutes the second chapter, which examines how the theatrical devices of the 1988 play . . . *Y a otra cosa mariposa* process homosexual desire and naturalize it. This experimental drama deploys a transvestite index in order to create a theatrical dislocation that destabilizes gender categories. It "normalizes" homosexuality within the prevailing social codes, forges a deconstruction of heterosexuality and entertains a competing homosexual discourse. While the play evolves within a specifically Argentine context, evidenced for example by the ironic feminist appropriation of tangos, the subject matter of this piece is less regionally specific than the Brazilian and North American examples. Unlike the Brazilian case study, which seeks to problematize universal notions of universality among women, the Argentine play is predicated, precisely, on the ontological presupposition of "Woman" as a universal sign. The commonality among women is founded exclusively on their sexual desire. Important aspects that differentiate women, such as social class, race, ethnicity, cultural and linguistic variations, are erased in the construction of all-encompassing theoretical assumptions.

The third chapter examines *Cocinar hombres*, a Mexican experimental piece. The feminist ideology that the play incarnates is manifested through the issues it stages: women's desire, women's sexuality, the flight to a world inhabited only by women, and the construction of a language. A "feminine" stage space and dramatic time departs notoriously from conventional dramatic forms and open up the possibility of reading the play as representative of "feminine dramaturgy." Like the Argentine case study, the feminist vision of Carmen Boullosa's *Cocinar hombres* is incarnated in a radical version of feminism in which women's primary relationship is with other women. Difference is framed in the sameness defined by women's separation from men, so that a new monolith is erected from which it is difficult to deviate. Variations of class, race, and culture among women are not accounted for.

The fourth chapter dramatizes the gestation of a bilingual/bicultural identity within the American context. In form and content the play examined, *Simply María or the American Dream*, borrows from Mexican and North American popular culture. It subverts these appropriations, producing a new creation that destabilizes both cultural systems, yet designs a space of its own. The play adopts a Brechtian format that is "Chicanized" to fit the subversive character of the play. It invites a closer examination of race and class issues as they affect the construction of this new identity and its representation. In contrast to the Brazilian example, U.S. Latinas, like other women of color in the North America context, struggle to attain agency, equality, justice and interpretative power.

In Spain during the Renaissance, Calderón de la Barca wrote *El gran teatro del mundo*, a Christian allegory of humanity's "performance" on earth; in the meantime, in Italy Machiavelli formulated a "script" to be "performed" by his prince ruler—an actor. The metaphors of life as theater, of the theatrical quality of life, and "acting" as a way of performing power are not products of our times. The difference nowadays is that "marginal actors," among them ethnic women of working-class background and emancipatory politics, cognizant of the constructed nature of power, are contesting the principal actors' "performances of power." This study is a performance of feminism from the margins to the center.[13]

Chapter 1: Dirt and Domesticity: Constructions of "Race" and Gender in Contemporary Brazilian Theater

Brazilian Women Playwrights and Theater Histories

Theater in Brazil traces its beginnings to the plays brought from Portugal by Christian missionaries. Since then, Brazilian theater has experienced periods of splendid artistic growth and experimentation, as well as trying times in which the theater was in danger of extinction or stagnation. While the history of Brazilian drama is rich for its abundance, women playwrights, as in most literary traditions, are conspicuously absent. The project of reconstructing a record of theater written by women encounters several research limitations: a sampling of most Brazilian literary histories demonstrates that less attention is paid to documenting the trajectory of drama as opposed to the other genres, which, of course, is true of other countries as well. Further, when an author has written plays but is better known for her/his narrative or poetic writings, the plays are often mentioned only in passing or take on interest because of the writer's fame as a novelist (witness the cases of Fuentes, Puig, and Vargas Llosa). Rarely is a conscious effort made to investigate how these plays are related to the rest of the author's literary production. I cite, for instance, the recently updated version of *História concisa da literatura brasileira,* considered by many specialists in the field as the best survey of its sort. Its author, Alfredo Bosi, is one of Brazil's highly respected critics and a professor of Brazilian literature at that country's most prestigious institution, the Universidade de São Paulo. Bosi's *História* is a fine literary history that demonstrates breadth of knowledge and clear prose; yet, it pays but marginal attention to theater, and the number of women writers cited is scanty. Of the women noted, a few, aside from devoting themselves to narrative or poetic forms, also wrote plays. Among them is the first woman invited to be a member of the Brazilian Academy of Letters, Rachel de Queiroz, whose plays, *Lampião* (1953) and *A beata Maria do Egito* (1958), are overshadowed by Queiroz's narrative. Whether the dramatic genre was just a phase of Queiroz's literary exploration, or whether poor reception of the author's dramatic pieces motivated her to discontinue experimenting with this genre are questions inadvertently silenced by literary historians and critics. In general, strides in the field of theater are seen as secondary to the development of the female author and marginal to the course of Brazilian literary history.

To find more information on women who have written plays, one needs to turn to theater histories, but even there the information is sparse. Lothar Hessel's and Georges Readers' *O teatro no Brasil sob Dom Pedro II* (1986) does register the accomplishment of Brazil's first published woman playwright, Maria Angélica Ribeiro (1829-1880), and her outcry at society's biases towards women playwrights: initial steps in this field were dismissed on the grounds that playwriting was a male enterprise (27). Aside from Ribeiro, no other woman is mentioned in this study. Moreover, in examining many studies that cover Brazilian theater history from its beginnings to the end of the last century, I did not find any other woman cited. Women playwrights during the first half of this century receive equally meager notice. Then, in 1965, Luiza Barreto Leite publishes *A mulher no teatro brasileiro*. From the perspective of a North American feminist critic writing in the '90s, this study perpetuates men's patriarchal value judgements and their expectations of women's capabilities. Barreto's book is not a study of women playwrights but rather a survey of women's participation in the theater as actresses, a presence in the theater that Barreto celebrates as an example of women's talents and originality. Further, when the author asserts that "No terreno da criação as mulheres, pouco numerosas, são ainda mais fracas, literária e tecnicamente" (10), she unquestionably espouses male criteria. Only two women are exempt from this judgement: Maria Clara, author of children's theater, and Chiquinha Gonzaga, composer of musical scores for dramatic performances. Beyond documenting their names, Barreto does not discuss the work of these women in any detail; she does not even convey the chronological context that would give a reader unfamiliar with this field an idea of the period in which these two authors lived. Perhaps the emphasis on recording the achievement of actresses on the Brazilian stage stems from Barreto's own background as an actress and founder of the group "Os Comediantes." But her perspective may also be skewed by the long tradition that has welcomed women's participation on the stage as actresses rather than as playwrights.

Significantly, the newspaper articles written for *O Estado de São Paulo*, "A arte de quatro mulheres nos palcos do Rio" (1983) and "A mulher no palco" (1985), insinuate that women's status in the theater did not change greatly since 1965. Like Barreto's work, these essays praise women's presence on the stage. The 1985 publication states: "Durante os 150 anos do teatro brasileiro, a presença feminina tem sido preponderante. E, em algumas ocasiões, como agora, elas são donas dos principais espectáculos que estão sendo apresentados" (10). While at one point this report claims women hold center position in dramatic productions as stage managers, directors, and playwrights, the article mentions only one playwright and no woman stage manager or director. Surveying instead prominent actresses, the essay discloses the title of some of the plays in which they appeared: *Frankenstein, Cyrano de Bergerac,* and *Santa Joana.* Aside from *Santa Joana,* these dramatic pieces have males as leading characters; while the presence of women characters is important to the development of the plot, their existence pivots around the male protagonist. Thus, when women appear on the Brazilian stage in roles worthy of critics' attention, they do so by representing characters that comply with the manner in which Western civilization has constructed women for and by the visual pleasure of men's gaze and desire. It is telling, for example, that the report's choice of actresses is not reflective of Brazil's multiracial society: all the performers mentioned in the article are white Brazilians who fit a European model of women's beauty. Given that Brazil's historical and current reality is multiracial, one is compelled to wonder what the absence of women of color on the Brazilian stage intimates about that society. Furthermore, if the article is correct in stating that women are dominating the stage on all levels, what justifies the selection of only one female playwright, Leilah Assunção? What explains the existence of a book that traces the career of Brazilian actress Cacilda Becker but one, to date, that investigates women playwrights or plays written by women who, for a short period during their careers, experimented with the dramatic genre? In some respects, there is little difference between this article written by a male journalist and Barreto's study written twenty years earlier.

Contemporary Women Playwrights

The year 1969 witnessed the emergence of several women who wrote especially for the theater, among them Leilah Assunção, Consuelo de Castro, Renata Pallottini, Hilda Hilst, and Isabel Câmara; in the late seventies, Maria Adelaide Amaral joined the group of contemporary dramatists.[1] These playwrights appeared during the difficult period of the country's second dictatorship in this century; both Assunção and Castro had some of their early plays censored. The government that came to power in 1964 advanced the protection of "national security" as a recourse to launch systematic censorship of anything that could suggest even slightly a critique of the regime's ideal of social and political order. Article 41 of decree 20,493 contained the regulations that bowdlerize theatrical activity. Three of the eight clauses of these laws suffice to intimate how the vague wording of the statements fostered extremely subjective interpretations: "Será negada autorização sempre que o texto: a) Contiver qualquer ofensa ao decoro público; b) Divulgar ou induzir aos maus costumes; c) Ferir de qualquer forma, a dignidade dos interesses nacionais." The definition of "decoro público," "maus costumes," and "a dignidade dos interesses nacionais" is left to the discretion of the censor. As is invariably the way of censorship, between 1964 and 1979 this law led to the expurgation of a great number of plays, and of those plays that were allowed to be performed on stage, the content was often altered to comply with the demands of the state. While article 41 policed the maintenance of order in regards to theatrical performance, the extension of censorship to other forms of communication such as newspapers, journals, and books was institutionalized in 1970 through article 1,077, which prohibited any medium of communication perceived by the government as a potential threat to national security or contrary to morality and good customs. These government restrictions framed what became known as the years of "linha dura." In *O palco amordaçado,* Brazilian theater critic Yan Michalski records in detail the effects of censorship on dramatic performances.

Other less tangible but equally important consequences surfaced in the literary production of this period as well. A general thematic overview of Brazilian plays written during the dictatorship reveals a predilection for themes that involved the individual as a lone figure in conflict with society. This concern, of course, is not uniquely Brazilian nor exclusive to this century, but its salient presence during the years of the "linha dura" insinuates that Brazilian playwrights felt a particular urgency to represent this theme—not surprisingly, since for some playwrights this was an expression of their desire to understand, explain, and denounce the prevailing political condition. Consequently, most of the plays written during this period are less concerned with theatrical experiment for its own sake; the realist dramatic form is the most commonly employed by playwrights of both sexes.

Sensitive to their historical reality, the Brazilian women dramatists who wrote during the military dictatorship did not make the development of an essentialist female dramatic aesthetic their priority. Instead, they chose to concentrate on pressing social issues as in the case of Castro or, like Assunção, on subtle critiques of the social situation of middle-class women. Rather than implying that this orientation is a deficiency or an instance of underdevelopment, I wish to stress the importance of recognizing how political conditions influenced the choices and priorities of women writers. Under the social and political conditions prevalent in Brazil, an exclusive preoccupation with gender issues and the development of a female dramatic aesthetic were concerns less pressing for these women playwrights than for writers from democratic, stable, and prosperous nations. Once military rule is lifted and a freer social and artistic climate sets in, Castro, for example, began to bring to the forefront of her work the investigation of existential dilemmas that affect women's subjectivities.

3 Contemporary Brazilian Plays in Bilingual Edition offers English versions of plays by Assunção and Castro. Published in 1988, this volume is the first appearance with a North American publishing house of English translations of plays by Castro and Assunção. *Aviso prévio* is Consuelo de Castro's text included in this edition. Of all of Castro's work, this play is the least concerned with representing social issues in a realist form. Structurally this piece is experimental, and in regards to content it is existential, delving into woman's questioning of herself. Thus, it carries a universal theme detached from any specific Brazilian context and for that reason is more likely to attract audiences beyond its national borders.

The work of Assunção and Castro is not entirely unknown to North American theater researchers interested in Brazilian theater. As early as 1976, the *Latin American Theatre Review* published "A situação social da mulher no teatro de Consuelo de Castro e Leilah Assunção" by Alcides João de Barros, then a graduate student at the Universidade de São Paulo. The potential readership of this article is limited by its being written in Portuguese. Unlike the study by Barreto and the articles in *O Estado de São Paulo,* Barros documents the presence of women on the stage but qualifies this statement by admitting:

> Muitas são as mulheres que se dedicam a essa atividade em caráter professional, as vezes com invejável exito. Não se pode, entretanto, dizer o mesmo com relação as autoras de textos teatrais, pois

emboranão haja nenhuma objeção que as mulheres escrevam para o teatro, são raríssimas as que fazem, em comparação com os homens. (13)

According to this article, Castro's and Assunção's greatest contribution to the Brazilian stage is their "feminine" vision of facts and events that male playwrights had previously ignored. Aside from providing biographical information on Assunção and Castro, Barros traces each playwright's professional accomplishments—plays published, honors, translations, and productions abroad. One important distinction that he draws between Assunção and Castro is their undergraduate training. While both playwrights attended the Universidade de São Paulo, Assunção focused her studies on the field of education; Castro's acute social vision stems from her majoring in the social sciences, particularly political science and sociology (17). This sensitivity to social issues is evidenced in Castro's choice of dramatic themes: in her first play, *A prova da fogo ou invasão dos bárbaros* (1968), she deals with the 1968 campus student movement's confrontations with the police. While the protagonists of this play advanced social revolutionary aims as their goal, its ending in useless destruction points to the weakness of this group's commitments to radical aims, such as gender equality. This condemnation stems from the male students' inability to treat the women involved in the movement with equality: the men enjoy sexual freedom, leaving pregnant lovers behind; the women involved with them pay grave consequences. One pregnant woman is expelled from her parents' household; another woman's engagement is broken when her fiancé discovers that she had a brief earlier affair. The male students' rhetoric of revolution seems liberating, but it is not applicable to the double standards Brazilian society imposes upon women. The consequences women must suffer when they have no recourse but ill-induced abortions constitute the plot of another of this author's plays, *O porco ensanguentado*. The trajectory of Castro's work reveals a predisposition for themes that involve the predicament of women in a broad context of social relations. Brazilian theater critics, in general, have received Consuelo de Castro's work warmly.

For a North American critic who ventures to South America to research Brazilian theater, the task of finding information about women playwrights proves challenging. In São Paulo, for example, the Museu Lasar Segall houses the most complete collection of Brazilian theater; yet its archives hold only two plays each by Isabel Câmara and Maria

Adelaide Amaral. No other information about them or their work is available, and while their names appear sporadically in studies of contemporary theater, none of these discuss their work in any detail until the recent study by Elza Cunha de Vincenzo, *Um teatro da mulher: dramaturgia feminina no palco brasileiro contemporâneo.* A student of the dramatist and poet Renata Pallottini and a member of the faculty of the Universidade de São Paulo, Cunha de Vincenzo begins with a discussion of Brazil's difficult political period and later focuses on the pioneering work of Renata Pallottini and Hilda Hilts. The rest of the study is devoted to the dramatic production of Assunção, Castro, de Amaral, and Câmara. A dramatist not mentioned in Cunha de Vincenzo's work but who should be added is Rosana Hill. *S.O.S. é uma lésbica* (1980), a short one-act piece written by Hill, is a straightforward plea for equal human rights for lesbians and, as such, Brazil's first dramatic performance that openly deals with homosexuality, an issue that until then had been treated only indirectly. It is safe to say, in short, that Brazilian women dramatists have introduced to the stage new visions and concerns previously marginalized or completely ignored.

Race-ing and En-gendering the Domestic Sphere. Leilah Assunção, more than any other woman playwright, has contributed to changing Brazilian dramaturgy. Maria de Lourdes Torres Assunção's roots are traced to an interior city of the state of São Paulo. The daughter and granddaughter of prominent educators of her hometown of Botucatu, Leilah majored in education. Her artistic inclinations date to her early teens when she began writing fiction. Later, while a university student in São Paulo, Leilah developed her interests in acting and playwriting through theater studies with the prominent dramaturg Eugênio Kusnet in his theatrical company *Teatro Oficina.* Before devoting herself entirely to writing, Leilah worked for a brief period as a high fashion model in Europe and upon her return to Brazil as an actress for the theater and television. In 1964, with her television script, *Vejo um vulto na janela, me acudam que eu sou donzela,* Assunção initiated her professional writing career. Five years later she published her first play, *Fala baixo, senão eu grito;* since then, Assunção's career as a playwright has been steadily fruitful. The television scripts she has written in addition to plays have allowed her to reach a larger audience and to gain a national and international notoriety that has escaped other women dramatists. Moreover, Assunção's involvement in enterprises that support the growth of women artists, such as the 1980s project "Espaço/arte: mulher," a multiartistic exhibition of Brazilian women's creative work, has contributed to her prominence in the Brazilian artistic and cultural world (24). While she actively promotes the work of women artists, Assunção insists she is not a feminist, viewing labels as dogmatic and ideologically limiting. Still, since the first play to the latest, her theatrical production shows a predilection for dealing with issues that concern the lives of women and for dramatizing the way rigid social structures curtail the development of a genuinely humane and equitable society for both sexes. In a recent interview, Assunção explains her position:

> ... Tanto que agora eu falo que eu fui pre-feminista e pós-feminista, então eu nunca fui feminista. Esse problema do termo feminista. E lógico que toda minha obra é feminista. Não tem como negar. Eu sei que não sou feminista. Toda minha posição na vida é feminista no sentido de reinvindicar, de lutar pelas mulheres. (PI)

As in Argentina, feminism in Brazil has been frequently associated with antimale, antifamily, and lesbian positions and is considered a movement that in the 1990s lacks currency and constituency. When asked why she writes for the theater, Assunção responds:

> É minha forma de me comunicar e dizer as coisas que me incomodam. Porque as coisas que me incomodam, e não disser apenas as que me faz sofrer . . . as coisas que são injustas e o ser humano que eu vejo que sofre mais que eu, que é mais maltratado pela opressão, pela injustiça, essa distribução de riqueza no Brasil que é uma verdadeira barbaridadade... a opressão não só da mulher como a do preto, a do operario, a da criança abandonada no Brasil. (PI)

As the analysis that follows indicates, these "coisas que me incomodam" are the raw material of Assunção's theater.

Simone de Beauvoir's proposition in *The Second Sex* that women are largely made "feminine" through social interaction, and not simply born that way, had an electrifying effect on the emerging American feminist movement of the late 1950s and early 1960s. Using Beauvoir's insights, feminists developed the concept of gender to describe behavior which could be attributed to cultural training rather than biology, as had been previously theorized. This meant that so-called feminine traits could be seen as historically and socially constructed rather than innate. Theories of behavior also encompassed issues of class, race, and the operations of ideology, all of which had a direct impact on the associations of women with the space and labor of the home. Traditionally, the burdens of earning a good living to support a wife and children fall exclusively upon men; in exchange for the freedom from this obligation, women must stay home to "keep the house." In this system, the home becomes for women a powerful, contradictory metaphor: it is often the site of abuse, disenfranchisement, and fulfillment.

Operative to our days is the prevalent conception of the essentially feminine nature of the home and domestic chores. The ramifications of industrialization in the division of labor provide a context for understanding the history of the domestic enterprise. In a 1903 analysis of housework, historian Charlotte Gilman noted:

> The phrase "domestic work" does not apply to a special kind of work, but to a certain grade of work, a stage of development to which all kinds of works pass. All industries were once "domestic," that is, were performed at home and in the interest of the family. All industries have since that remote period risen to higher stages, except one or two which have never left their primal stage. (qtd. in Mertes 61)

As industries moved away from the domestic space, the new economic system dictated that domestic household labor was a job not worthy of a salary. During this period of industrial growth divisions of space and labor were solidified along lines of gender, class, and race. The private domestic space auspiced tasks like child rearing and home maintenance, domains reserved for the feminine sex. The feminization of the domestic space is critical to the development of the play *Lua nua* (1987) for its dramatization of the predicament of a Brazilian middle-class couple's professional and domestic arrangements. In the first part of my analysis, I will illustrate how Assunção insinuates that gendered behavior is a social construct that affects women as well as men. Secondly, I will investigate how domestic arrangements are symbolic of power relations that cross gender, class, and racial lines. In *Lua nua* the symbolic enactment of power relations is manifested on two levels: 1) On the domestic arrangement between husband and wife where the domestic sphere is feminized and the professional, public sphere is masculinized; 2) And, in the analysis of the conflicted relationship of dependency between the white, professional, middle-class employer and her working-class, colored maid, where one can see how within the domestic domain, there are additional levels of inferiority. This line of inquiry allows one to discern the ways in which the concepts of dirt and cleanliness are negotiated to define hierarchical distinctions within the definition of femininity. This symbolic relationship becomes crucial when one considers how class and race privilege are inscribed into concepts of cleanliness. Thus, within the domestic domain the individual who performs the dirtiest domestic chores is racialized to the lowest denominator. Extrapolating from the analysis of this play and its reception in Brazilian theater circles, I argue that Assunção introduces the domestic enterprise service to challenge simple notions of woman as a homogenous category united by common oppression and sisterhood; by dramatizing how race and class privilege differentiate women, it questions the notion of women as a universal: Brazil continues to maintain a social and economic system in which people of color—women of working-class background—are denied agency, equal representation, and, most importantly, humanity. Finally, the caricature-like construction of the maid raises further questions concerning women and representation: How do women with interpretative power represent race?

The exemplary middle-class couple of *Lua nua* is formed by a professional and working mother, Sílvia, an attorney who, although she has a maid to help her with the household chores, carries the full responsibilities involved with parenting and managing the domestic affairs, while her husband, Lúcio, an engineer, disengaged completely from responsibility for the household, behaves as if his salary alone maintains their home. As in another of Assunção's plays, *Fala baixo,* the dramatic time of *Lua nua* is compressed to a few hours to accentuate further the conceptualization of the family's structure as a locus of "political struggle" (Hartmann). The play opens in the living room of what is described as a middle-class home. The couple read separate sections of the newspaper. Through their initial dialogue, the power struggle that besets this couple is delineated; the content of the news that each one reads to the other introduces two of the play's principal concerns: Sílvia reads out loud her husband's horoscope: "Hojé é um dia de profundas mudanças, mas que aparentemente . . ." (9). Irritated, Lúcio tells his wife to stop reading; seconds later, he imitates his wife's gesture: "Nossa! Escute isso: Oitenta porcento das mulheres na Africa de . . ." Sílvia responds to her husband in the exact manner he had displayed towards her: she orders Lúcio to stop reading the news for her. Contrary to appearances, that morning is not an ordinary one: both Sílvia and Lúcio have decisive career appointments scheduled at the same hour. After the birth of her child eight months ago, Sílvia has recently returned to work and is meeting with clients of a prospective trial case, whereas Lúcio has a business meeting that could lead to a career promotion with the opportunity to transfer to North America. This homespun setting stages a battle in which husband and wife will negotiate new definitions for their domestic and professional responsibilities and roles—the private and public spheres.

The argument continues with Lúcio's criticism of his wife's attire and of her delay in recovering the figure she had before the birth of their child. Even his secretary, Lúcio claims, looks like a Parisian model in comparison to Sílvia. Lúcio is referring to beauty standards which are expected to be complied with in order to maintain their position in society. In the Brazilian social system—as, to a culturally different degree, in the United States—women, most particularly middle-class professional women, are encouraged to uphold and imitate high fashion models' standards of beauty and attire. As Naomi Wolf concludes in *The Beauty Myth,* multinational cosmetic and fashion industries whose dictums transcend national borders create an ideal of a woman that, while impossible to achieve for the majority, all women are expected to emulate. Yet, in comparing the average North American woman to her counterpart in Brazil, one notices that the South American standards are far more rigid. North American women have more freedom to deviate from those expectations; from the Brazilian perspective, they seem sloppier, less preoccupied with esthetics, fashion, and the cult of their bodies—marking in this way a cultural difference between them.

Dulce, described as "uma mulatta exuberante, redonda e sensual" (10), and Sílvia engage in putting away the groceries, a task that makes evident that the person in charge of choosing the household goods is the maid. Between the "dona da casa" and the "empregada" exists a relationship of complicity and solidarity that brings them together: Dulce's trip to the supermarket was accompanied by Sílvia's request to deliver a note setting a date with a tennis player to whom Dulce refers as "o moço do carro vermelho" (16). This scene suggests that Sílvia is entertaining the prospect of an extramarital affair that is being orchestrated primarily by Dulce. Sílvia's own distant and estranged relationship with her husband situates her in a vulnerable position, and she falls easily under Dulce's influence.

But the bonding between Dulce and Sílvia has several levels. It is not simply the case of extramarital conspiracies. Together, they share the burden of running the household, of taking care of the baby's needs. The domestic responsibilities make the two women akin in terms of female exploitation in a patriarchal society. Not only is Lúcio absent from participation in this realm, but he does not give credit to the work that Sílvia does. Lúcio's definition of a wife is equal to the responsibilities of the domestic help: ". . . Quem escolhe o que se come nesta casa? Quem organiza a roupa que eu visto, meus remédios? Quem cuida de *meu* filho, Sílvia? . . . Só falta mesmo eu dormir com esse carro alegórico [Dulce] para me sentir casado com ele!" (25). Lúcio's relationship with his wife is victimizing and full of contradictions. At times, he affirms that, in contradistinction to his colleague who is married to a "datilógrafa," he is proud his wife is an attorney. But when Sílvia attempts to assert the importance of her professional commitments, Lúcio ignores her career responsibilities, dismissing Sílvia's profession as an obstacle to the fulfillment of her duties as a wife and mother. In both the professional and domestic levels, Lúcio fails to acknowledge Sílvia's contributions. In this instance, Lúcio embodies the attitude that many Brazilian men, to this day, maintain in regards to their wives' professions, which are invariably seen as less important, less serious than their own.[2] Lúcio, for example, insists that his wife abandon her profession. He seems unaware that, if they are to maintain their class standing, both salaries are needed. Although described as "ascendent clásse méia," this couple experiences difficulties in making ends meet, for, among other things, Lúcio has to forgo his English classes and Sílvia does not frequent a salon for her beauty needs; instead, she manages by doing things herself at home.

    Because both women, to various degrees, participate in domestic affairs, Dulce has the latitude to be disrespectful toward her "patroa." Their bonding is predicated on their both being participants of the domestic sphere, of their being born into an unequal social system that relegates their gender to an inferior status. When Sílvia finally confronts her maid about the liberties Dulce assumes in her job, such as lying about the death of a relative in order to take time off from work or "borrowing" Silvia's underwear without asking for permission or buying extra things for herself with the household money, Dulce responds by challenging Silvia's status as the "patroa":

> Patrão é quem não mexe no lixo. O Seu Lúcio jamais limpou nem vai limpar o Júnior. Por isso ele me despreza mais eu respeito ele. A

> Senhora, Dona Sílvia, me desculpa, mais se eu sou lixo, a senhora é
> tão lixo quanto eu. (32)

To varying degrees, both women are involved in manual activities that historically have been executed by hired hands. Furthermore, Dulce's words allude to the "feminization" associated with the cultural constructions of dirt and cleanliness as they evoke a set of class and, in this case as well, race relations. Anthropologists have pointed to the different ways in which dirt has been negotiated to suggest hierarchical distinctions within definitions of femininity. The symbolic relationship between dirt and the body of the servant is crucial in order to maintain racial and class privilege. Dirt functions as a social and cultural construction that designates the lower class (Ward 6-8). In this case, that order has been destabilized because the employer's economic situation has forced Sílvia to "get dirty" by participating in domestic activities. In doing so, Sílvia, in the eyes of Dulce, has demeaned herself to the level of a domestic. Dulce's affirmation illustrates her unquestioned acceptance of an ideology that relegates domestic work, the source of her sense of self, to garbage.

The argument between "patroa" and "empregada" reaches a climax when Dulce challenges Sílvia's maternal commitments: ". . . O Júnior pode ter saído da sua [barriga]. Mais a mãe dele mesmo, de verdade, dia-a-dia sou eu. Dona Sílvia me desculpa, mas a mãe de seu filho sou eu" (33). Sílvia responds with a gesture that reminds us of the visual semiotic elements of the theatrical performance: she calmly takes off her house slippers and puts on her high heels (although dressed for work since the opening of the play, Sílvia, up to this moment, had been wearing slippers). Distancing herself from the domestic realm and, thus, from Dulce and with the assurance that her professional status carries, Sílvia fires Dulce from her job. The dismissal is effective immediately. There is no point in arguing about it, Sílvia affirms. A feminist materialist interpretation of this confrontation would claim that in a hierarchical capitalist society, economic class differences are an impediment for the development of genuine solidarity among women (Case 90).

With the maid out of the scene, Sílvia is forced to confront Lúcio about the sexual division of domestic labor. When Lúcio returns to pick up Sílvia and drive her to work, she informs him that she fired the maid:

> LUCIO É um problema mesmo . . . Só que eu estou atrasadíssimo, depois você me liga para dizer como é que resolveu por hoje.
> SILVIA Espera aí Lúcio. Acho que você não entendeu ainda. A saída da Dulce é um problema nosso e não apenas meu.
> LUCIO Mais foi você que despediu a moça, voce causou o problema, agora resolva você, ora!
> SILVIA Ela estrapolou todos os limites, poderia ter sido com você, é como se ela tivesse . . . pedido demissão. É um problema de nossa casa a ser resolvido, portanto, conjuntamente.
> LUCIO Só que eu tenho a entrevista com os americanos às dez e meia e estou atrasado!
> SILVIA Mas eu também tenho uma entrevista às dez e meia . . .
> LUCIO Ah! Você não vai querer me comparar agora essa sua entrevista com o meu trabalho, vai? . . . Sílvia, é claro que minha entrevista é muito mais importante. (35)

In this case, Assunção reminds the Brazilian spectators of how the reality of the play and of Brazilian contemporary society corresponds with Moema Toscano's affirmation: "Enquanto não se superar a necessidade da empregada doméstica (como acontece nos países desenvolvidos), eu não acredito que possa haver um feminismo no Brasil" (qtd. in Fagundes 110). For it is Dulce's absence that inevitably leads Sílvia to confront her husband about the unequal domestic arragements. When Lúcio begins to exit the living room towards the street, Sílvia proceeds in the same fashion, making it clear that she is determined to stop carrying the domestic responsibilities all on her own. Initially, Lúcio interprets Sílvia's behavior as a childish game, but he is not exempted from listening to Sílvia's arguments as she asserts that, if need be, she will have recourse to a divorce: ". . . Eu preciso de uma esposa e não dum marido. . ." (48).

Sílvia continues with a resounding echo of the problems faced today by many middle-class professional women, not just in Brazil:

> . . . Tenho o escritório, a casa, o Júnior, o regime-sempre-linda-e-cheirosa-senão-perde-o-marido, trabalhar e não comer, e a bendita criança chora, a trabalhar e não dormir, maldito choro, mal-di-ta criança. Ah não foi meu seio que perdeu o atrevimento, não, fui eu, inteira, eu vi no espelho, é questão de postura, estou arcada, como se carregasse o mundo nas minhas costas! Você dorme de noite e tem fim de semana, a Dulce também tem fim de semana Eu *nunca*! Nem férias! Eu não sou Deus mes-mo! Eu e Ele fizemos o mundo juntos sim, em seis dias. Mais Ele, o Senhor, no sétimo descansou! . . . (48)

The hour of their meetings is drawing closer, and for the first time Lúcio addresses their domestic dilemma in the plural form: "não podemos nos atrasar" (49). Accompanying these words with the gesture of initiating the task of preparing the baby's bottle, Lúcio reminds Sílvia that if he does not help with household chores it is because she does not allow him to do it: implying that Sílvia is embarrassed to have her husband involved in domestic affairs; this would translate into a feminization of an individual expected to uphold masculinity in their household. This passage reveals the dominant's culture manipulation of the domestic as a function only women can perform easily and well. Furthermore, it also highlights the ways in which women inadvertently support unequal divisions of domestic labor. On another level, it reminds us that just like feminine comportment, masculine behavior is socially constructed.

The next scene finds Lúcio celebrating Sílvia's career because she, unlike him, is enacting in her professional choice a true vocation. At this point, Lúcio reveals his dissatisfaction with his engineering job, a profession he chose motivated by a desire to achieve economic security, that is, knowing that as a man he would be expected to be a stable breadwinner. But just as Lúcio, for the first time, expresses his support of his wife's aspirations, Sílvia acknowledges the deep inner satisfaction that motherhood has added to her life. She recalls her wish that her husband, not her maid, should have shared with her the moment of that illuminating discovery. Hence, the plays captures the traditional "masculinization" of the public space and the "femininization" of the domestic. Having overheard Sílvia's retelling of that incident, Dulce returns to the scene, sobbing, moved by Sílvia's story. After apologizing for their behavior, Dulce volunteers to stay with the baby so that the couple may go to their meetings.

The two women's participation in the domestic space in *Lua nua* is precisely what makes their relationship worth a closer examination. If one centers on the character of Sílvia, this play would fit the description of a feminist text. While Sílvia is not a faultless heroine, she is, nonetheless, thrust into a situation that coerces her to assert herself and to alter an unfair domestic arrangement; on this level, *Lua nua* can be read as embracing a feminist concern. While Dulce is not the principal character, her strategic presence and absence from the action propels climactic, decisive moments. However, a striking feature of Dulce is her caricature-like construction. Described as an exuberant, curvy, sensual mulatta, Dulce dresses in low-cut blouses that accentuate her physique. Her sensuality is highlighted by the attention the men in the neighborhood—from the pharmacist to the milkman—pay to Dulce's physical attributes. Implicitly, it is under Dulce's influence that Sílvia begins to entertain the prospect of an extramarital affair; Dulce's overflowing sensuality seems to impinge upon her "patrão." Yet, these characteristics are all in accordance with an ideology that constructed working-class women, and especially women of color, as the repositories of sexuality and of moral laxity (inferiority).[3] Sílvia may marginally participate in household chores, but Dulce is the one who contains the "psychological and moral dirt" of the household. In this way, the higher social status and qualitative superiority of Sílvia are never truly challenged.

Women of African descent have historically been represented in literature as sexual objects. In this case, Assunção ironically perpetuates common stereotypes. Homi K. Bhabha writes:

> Skin, as the key signifier of cultural and racial difference in the stereotype, is the most visible of fetishes, recognized as common knowledge in a range of cultural, political, historical discourses, and plays a public part in the racial drama that is enacted every day in colonial societies. (82)

Dulce's African extraction is played out on several levels: 1) as is expected, Dulce dances with great rhythm and sensuality, an activity Sílvia does not imitate well because she is white and therefore, presumably, is not biologically endowed to be equally rhythmic and sensual; 2) Dulce has internalized racism to the extreme of being ashamed of her African heritage. On one occasion, Sílvia asks Dulce to teach her to dance: "Dança lá dos teus antepassados, de tua bisavó, princesa linda raptada do coração da Africa." Dulce responds by asking: "Mas ninguém diz que sou neta de avó preta diz? Diz?" (21); and 3) Dulce is guilty of lying and stealing, a common complaint voiced by middle-class Brazilian "patroãs" of their lower-class "empregadas". It is difficult to separate class and race in a society in which the lower classes are composed of those closer to African ties. In Brazil there is still a strong correlation between race and social standing: most whites are at the top, most blacks are at the bottom, and mixed bloods largely in between (Skidmore 154).

In a North American setting, it is difficult to conceive that the characterization of Dulce would have not met with public uproar from the African-American community and other ethnic minority groups.

Throughout the play, Lúcio constantly dehumanizes Dulce by associating her with the bestial world: he calls her cousin of a cow with cloven hoofs. The animal-like innuendoes are akin to the etymology of the term mulatta—a hybrid animal similar to a mule (Stephens 169). The objectified, bestial codification of Afro-Brazilians is reflective of the ideology used to justify African slavery. Lúcio's description of Dulce as "uma boba alegre que nasceu para cumprir ordens" (23) is an indication that, in terms of race, the dominant group has retained a master's mentality in its treatment of Afro-Brazilians.

Significantly, in 1944, the short-lived Teatro Experimental do Negro (TEN) was founded in Rio de Janeiro with the purpose of creating a black theater that would openly challenge a theatrical tradition that relegated Afro-Brazilians to inferior, stereotyped roles such as the fool, clown, idler, humble domestic, or eternal slave (Turner 33). Forty-two years later, Dulce incarnates the sort of demeaning role TEN strove to eradicate. Furthermore, to justify the servant's condition as natural and permanent, the play's recourse is to advance pseudoscientific literature that Brazilian white society has historically used to legitimize the Afro-Brazilians' condition: *Lua nua* begins with a newspaper's allusion to African women. Yet, on that occasion, the contents of those news are not disclosed. While arguing with Dulce, Sílvia's sense of superiority is enhanced by the power she has in revealing the contemporary condition of women in Africa:

> Dulce, Dulce, sua idiota! Sua bisavó que voava linda no coração da África, sabe o que fizeram com ela? Sabe? . . . "Oitenta porcento das mulheres na África da influência muçulmana tem o sexo cortado" . . . Não sonho não: é isso mesmo que você escutou: ho-je; o sexo cor-ta-do, sabe o que é isso? . . . Você nasceu para isso mesmo, para limpar toda a minha roupa suja. E com isso poupar as minhas mãos cuidadas de se lambuzarem no tanque. (32)

Sílvia's revelation is intended to make Dulce think her subservient position in Brazilian society is, in fact, a privileged condition. Judith Rollins terms "maternalism" the type of rationalization that advances the idea that the employer is doing her maid a favor by "giving" her work, that in so doing she is protecting and sponsoring the less fortunate (155-203). From a feminist materialist position, the "mothering" role is an extension of the domestic sphere that has been culturally induced by society and has contributed to women's historical exclusion from the public sphere (Case 85).

As represented in this play, Brazilian society offers little indication of aspiring to racial and class equity. In the ironic final scene Dulce opens the windows, and, looking at the street, she sighs emotionally:

> Ah, meus orixás, por favor . . . Vê se faz passar aí na frente, pra sacudir a minha vida agora . . . Um moço de carro vermelho . . . alto, de cabelo loiro, encaracolado . . . Montado num alazão doirado . . . .(54)

For oppressed individuals fantasy is the only way of coping with their realities. The possibility for change, the play suggests, is not open to everybody: for individuals of Dulce's racial and economic background, Brazilian society offers no hope for transcending their depressed situation. Nevertheless, Dulce's role is important because it fulfills the couple's middle-class need for "the self-enhancing satisfactions that emanate from having the presence of an inferior and validating the employers' lifestyle, ideology, and social world, from their familial interrelations to the economically and racially stratified system in which they live" (Steel 300). In light of this awareness, when one speaks of *Lua nua* as a "potentially" feminist play, one needs to ask for whom is feminism espoused in the play? While Dulce nurses her employer's baby so that Sílvia may participate in the public sphere, who attends to the servant's children? *Lua nua* is the first of Assunção plays to bring on stage an Afro-Brazilian woman.[4] Hence, recalling that theater can mirror society and that it has the potential to reshape society's image of itself the play dramatizes how tenuous middle-class women have their "freedom"; it also forces one to think of what does Dulce's characterization and fate reveal about Brazilian women of color?

Yet, the critical commentaries on *Lua nua* provide an indication of the participation of Afro-Brazilian women in the theater and, conversely, in society. Yan Michalski, the highly respected Brazilian theater critic, in the introduction to his edition of the play, notes:

> Ela é uma guerreira, como guerreiras são as suas oprimidas e libertárias heroínas . . . Em todas as suas peças a mulher luta por libertar-se do jogo que a sociedade dominada pelo homen lhe impõe . . . Mais do que feminista, esta é uma obra essencialmente humanista, que clama por um entendimento generoso e construtivo entre todos os habitantes do planeta. (5-6)

The absence of any remark that acknowledges the racist element of this play is striking but not surprising. One can assume that in Michalski's world view there is no room for Afro-Brazilians as "mulheres brasileiras" and "habitantes do planeta." Significantly, Elza Cunha de Vincenzo's *Um teatro da mulher* discusses how this play stages women's "dupla jornada," but, she, too, makes nothing of the racial and economic issues suggested by the play: she fails to see Dulce.

The failure to take note of the racial dimension of the play in 1987 is not new, for it is the same type of attitude that has led Brazilian theater historians to ignore the existence, well documented in Rio de Janeiro's and São Paulo's newspapers, of the Teatro Experimental Negro (Turner 35). Michalski repeats the gesture of his predecessors: he names the actress who plays Sílvia but does not mention the actress who represents Dulce. Similarly, Brazilians in the '40s and '50s received negatively TEN's efforts to affirm Afro-Brazilian values and black pride (Turner 40). Perhaps it should surprise no one that in Dulce's final scene she longs for a tall, blond man.[5] As a black woman in a society that denigrates colored people, Dulce is given few options but to desire that which she is not.

By addressing professional women's "dupla jornada de trabalho" and relating this issue particularly to the Brazilian context, where, unlike in North America, maids are an essential component of middle-class households, Assunção introduces the domestic service enterprise to challenge common notions of woman as a homogenous category united by a common oppression and sisterhood; she dramatizes the dramatic differences race and class make among women. Assunção is aware of her limitations as a writer when she confesses: "É claro que eu posso escrever uma peça a favor do negro, do menor abandonado y tudo isso; agora, eu nunca serei tão forte quanto uma negra escrevendo, como um negro escrevendo" (PI). The racial dimension of the play raises further questions concerning representation: what happens when women in power represent race? Do they fall into the same stereotypes that men have constructed about women?

While historically Latin American women writers, responding to their marginality in patriarchal societies, have shown a greater disposition than men to represent those who are further marginalized by racial and economic status, critics often leave unexamined the nature of that representation. Can a subaltern speak for the other? The interpretative power that in North America women of color—the Chicana Josefina López—for example, have achieved is still out of the reach of the majority of Afro-Brazilian women. But even for those few elite Brazilian women who have gained access to the interpretative sphere, the "dupla jornada de trabalho" continues to affect and limit their literary productivity. In *Lua nua,* Assunção brings all these concerns to the forefront of Brazilian theater; in doing so, she successfully uses her creativity to communicate "as coisas que me incomodam."

CHAPTER 2: (DE)NATURALIZING DESIRE: HOMOEROTICISM AND PERFORMANCE

> A woman shall not wear anything that pertains to a man, nor shall a man put on a woman's garment; for whoever does these things is an abomination to the Lord your God. (Deuteronomy 22.5)

> Sexual role-playing has implications for gender play: the way people perform their sexuality influences how they wear their gender . . . A body displayed in representation that belongs to the female gender class is assumed to be heterosexual, since male desire organizes the representational system. Disrupting the assumption of heterosexuality, and replacing male desire with lesbian desire, for example, offers radical readings of the meanings produced by representation. (Dolan 63)

Argentinean Women Playwrights:
Theater Histories and Contemporary Feminisms

The emergence of a national theater in Argentina is documented as early as the eighteenth century when theatrical performances celebrated the crowning of Spain's King Fernando VI. Prior to this time, as in the rest of the American continent, Spanish missionaries had utilized Christian plays to indoctrinate the indigenous populations. The trajectory of Argentine theater after the eighteenth century followed the same artistic patterns of the mother country, often adapting regional themes to Spanish comedies and *sainetes* or to plays that dramatized local historical events. Spanish touring companies worked in Buenos Aires, and frequently their principal actors and actresses did not return to Europe, opting, instead, to stay in Argentina.

As in the Brazilian case, Argentine theater histories record the presence of women as distinguished actresses who were commonly married to prominent directors of theater companies.[1] As writers, creators of dramatic texts, women are absent from most Argentine literary histories (Ordaz 1-8). One does not find nineteenth-century playwrights who are counterparts to the Brazilian María Angélica Ribeiro and the Cuban Gertrudis Gómez de Avellaneda. While feminist critics have rediscovered early twentieth-century Argentinean women writers like Alfonsina Storni, Alejandra Pizarnik, Silvina Ocampo, and María Elena

Walsh, none of these women experimented with dramatic writing. Many more years had to pass before an Argentine woman would attempt to use the stage to dramatize feminist concerns.

Griselda Gambaro undoubtedly ranks among the most commercially and critically successful playwrights of contemporary Latin American, specifically Argentinean, theater. For decades, she was frequently the only woman dramatist whose plays were produced either in Argentina and, while the author was in exile during the military rule, in European countries, for instance in Spain and France. Gambaro began writing for the theater in the late '60s, and with more than twenty plays to her credit, she is distinguished for the high quality of her prolific production. For many years, critics placed Gambaro's work in the vein of absurdist theater, failing to see that what appeared to be absurd plots, dialogue, and use of stage space were metaphors for the palpable realities of Argentinean society. The structures of oppression and repression, of persecution and aggression, are so inherent to life, that the cruelty and violence expressed in human relations in plays like *Los siameses, El desatino,* and *El campo* are not absurdist abstractions but theatrical metaphors responsive to the heightened quality of Argentine reality (Foster, *Cultural* 137-38).

Gambaro's position in regards to feminisms is grounded on what she views as "realistic" contexts. Like most women writers discussed in this study, Gambaro does not align herself with feminist politics, nor does she believe in a biologically determined "feminine writing," but, like other writers, she concedes:

> La contribución al teatro que podemos hacer las escritoras es independiente de nuestro sexo, y sin embargo, nacerá de nuestra identidad, que contiene el sexo naturalmente. Una escritora asume su identidad, esencialmente, en su vida personal y social, y por lo tanto, traducirá esa identidad implícitamente en todo lo que haga . . . Nuestra identidad nos viene de nuestra inserción en el mundo, de la mirada que lancemos a ese mundo intentando desentrañar sus riquezas, sus carencias, sus conflictos. (20)

Significantly, Gambaro is the playwright most often invoked as an influence and inspiration to the younger generation of Argentine women playwrights, Susana Torres Molina among them. Torres Molina, like Gambaro, situates her work in her contextual environment, in human "machista societies," where the confrontations between men and women are the daily norm. Some feminist critics of Gambaro's early plays, noticing the absence of women characters or the staging of weak female characters, criticized Gambaro's work for its lack of a feminist ideology or, at least, a feminine vision. But as the author has pointed out: "En las obras cuestionadas, el mundo de los hombres era un mundo marcado por la incomprensión, el egoísmo, la injusticia. Es el mundo donde 'viven' las mujeres" (21).

That "mundo donde viven las mujeres" is where women playwrights continue to find obstacles to entering the theatrical world. Torres Molina, for example, advanced in a personal interview that women dramatists in Argentina face the same difficulties as men in entering theater circles. Nevertheless, when pressed for explanations that would justify why so few women are actively writing for the theater, she acknowledged that it is still more difficult for women than it is for men to break into the professional theater world. Citing the "jornada dupla" of professional women—lack of support, motherhood, domestic responsibilities, precisely the issues dramatized in Assunção's *Lua nua*—Torres Molina conceded that women are still at a disadvantage in comparison to men. In regards to women's participation in Argentine theater circles, Torres Molina concludes:

> Casi en todas las direcciones, las comisiones de teatro, los jurados de teatro, bueno, siempre hay una predominancia enorme de hombres más que de mujeres, de diez hombres habrá siempre una mujer . . . Los centros donde se digitan las cosas siempre están tomados por hombres. (PI)

While Argentine women, based on their gender identity, are not excluded from the world of professional theater, their distance from the centers of power and decision-making continues to make women's career development in the theater difficult.[2]

When asked to comment on her future projects, Torres Molina responds in a 1994 interview:

> No sé . . . que no me basta lo material solamente, que no me basta sentir que acá uno está para asumir un personaje, para ser exitoso profesionalmente, para que te vaya bien económicamente, yo creo que la vida tiene otras búsquedas. A mí eso no me basta, me interesa mucho hacer de mi vida una obra de arte, para eso trabajo para ser útil. (PI)

The underpinning of Torres Molina's philosophical position towards life and art is often expressed by her involvement in community affairs.

Indeed, an important facet of Torres Molina is her commitment and her labor on behalf of social causes. Aside from artistic endeavors, she devotes part of her time to community work that links the social world with art. For years now, Torres Molina has taken her talents to marginal places, like prisons and hospitals with AIDS patients, where she teaches courses in the writing of drama.

Like Leilah Assunção, Torres Molina first entered the world of theater through a career as an actress; she initially became interested in acting and began taking lessons as an effort to overcome her personal shyness. This inclination to accept challenges valiantly is what inspired her to write her collection of erotic short stories, *Dueña y señora:*

> Si todos los hombres pueden escribir sobre sus fantasías y sus realidades al nivel erótico, al nivel sexual, ¿por qué la mujer no lo hace? Entonces, de ahí fueron inspirados mis cuentos, pero más que pensar ¡ah! bueno voy a escribir cuentos en donde estaba más puesto el acento en una búsqueda literaria, acá lo que estaba más puesto era una actitud más transgresora . . . de una decir, bueno yo como mujer también puedo permitirme eso. (PI)

What began as an attempt to overcome a personal inadequacy later spurred a desire to experiment with playwriting and subsequently led to a distinguished body of dramatic work. Torres Molina's literary and dramatic production shatters conventional expectations: her theater often adopts experimental forms, distant from realist conventions; her desire to challenge social norms is a central propeller of her work. Torres Molina's earliest play, *Extraño juguete* (1977), was followed by . . . *Y a otra cosa mariposa* (1982), a collaborative venture, *Inventario* (1984), *Espiral de fuego* (1985), a musical *Soles* (1987), *Amantísima* (1987), *Unión mística* (1991), *Canto de sirenas* (1992), and *Manifiesto* (1993). Always in the vanguard, Torres Molina with her first play, an experimental piece that stages the sexual repression of middle-class Argentine women, sets the tone for further transgressive work. In tune with its social context, *Unión mística* dramatizes a deadly union—the AIDS disease—between two women and their common lover. As the first in Argentina to stage the effects of this mortal disease that plagues the world, Torres Molina was at the forefront of her country's theater.

While in Mexico Carmen Boullosa circulates freely among both the literary establishment and the eccentric, marginal theater circles, Torres Molina's dramatic productions, in contrast, exist principally on the margins of commercial enterprises, in what is considered the "Off" theater circles of Buenos Aires. There, she has earned a respectable space for her work. In distinction to this more transgressive and experimental theater realm, the commercial houses predominantly stage European classics or North American Broadway productions, Neil Simon, for example, as well as other events that are lucrative because they are performed by well-known television and film actors.

Torres Molina points out in an interview that "En 1981 escribí una pieza atacando el machismo argentino, . . . *Y a otra cosa mariposa*" (Eidelberg 392). As in certain circles of the United States and Latin America, in Argentina feminism has been characterized as a dogmatic position stridently antimen and antifamily. Torres Molina, similar to Boullosa and Assunção, rejects identifying herself as a feminist, and because a feminist profile is linked to lesbianism, Torres Molina, as well as many other women, distances herself from this position. Since *Dueña y señora* contained one story that dealt with a lesbian relationship, Torres Molina has frequently been associated with a lesbian orientation she adamantly refutes (PI).

It may be worth noting that, to judge by her statements in our interview, Torres Molina's unwillingness to publicly assume a feminist position and her reluctance to grant that some of her work destabilizes heterosexual gender discourses is a reaction against negative criticism she received after the publication of her collection of erotic short stories. Notwithstanding Torres Molina's disavowal of feminist and homoerotic strains, . . . *Y a otra cosa mariposa* opens up far more frontiers than the author is willing to concede.

Homoeroticism and Performance in
. . . *Y a otra cosa mariposa*

> Perla: Los hombres tienen esa ventaja.
> Maggi: ¿Qué ventaja?
> Perla: La de moverse con tanta libertad sin que nadie piense mal.
> (*Extraño juguete* 33)

Much recent work by literary and cultural critics focuses on the construction of gender and on the "constructedness" (rather than the naturalness, literality, and biology, or essence) of male and female as culturally marked categories (Garber 47). The social fabrication of gender differences, as the history of Western culture attests, has been regulated by sumptuary laws and dress codes that determine which biological gender class, male or female, is allowed to wear which vestment. To violate these laws is to become a transgressor of social codes. The essence of theater, however, is, in fact, the mechanism of substitution: role-playing, improvisation, costume, and disguise are fundamental to dramatic representation (Garber 29).

In Torres Molina's *Extraño juguete,* the characters allude to an advantage men have over women, a socially fabricated leverage that will become a basic experimental trope of the later piece, . . . *Y a otra cosa mariposa,* in which the author's only stipulation is that its four male characters be played by women. Structural and thematic similarities between *Extraño juguete* and . . . *Y a otra cosa mariposa* include the metatheatrical device of a play within a play or, more correctly, of a text within a text, that is, the characters of the piece are assigned to act out other roles within the framework of the role they are playing. In this case, I read the cross-gendered performative requisite of . . . *Y a otra cosa* as the theatrical device that is significant for its shock value, by way of reversing the archaic Western theater—from the Greeks through Shakespeare—where only males are allowed on the stage.[3] Furthermore, by having women perform the roles of men lusting after women, it yields the foreshadowing of a homoerotic representation. . . . *Y a otra cosa mariposa* processes homosexual desire and naturalizes it. The play brings into motion a transvestite index to create a theatrical dislocation that destabilizes gender categories; it normalizes homosexuality within the prevailing social codes, forging a deconstruction of heterosexuality, and thus allows the presence of a competing homosexual discourse.

. . . *Y a otra cosa mariposa* is divided into five scenes that chronicle the life, from adolescence to old age, of its protagonists. A thematic emphasis on sexuality is traceable in Torres Molina's work, and . . .*Y a otra cosa mariposa*, like *Extraño juguete,* centers on the human expression of sexuality. In the latter, the protagonists, two sisters, engage in a persistent feud over the attempts by one sister to repress the other's expressions of female sexuality. . . . *Y a otra cosa mariposa,* for its part, can be described as the annals of its characters' sexual conquests. The titles of its segments evoke the sexual lineament of each life stage: "La prima," "Metejón," "Despedida de soltero," "Bulín," and "Toda una vida." The first segment captures the flirtation with familial sexual initiation by one of the four teen-age boys; "Metejón" recreates the playful nature of their sexual conquests as late teenagers; "Despedida de soltero" chronicles the protagonists in their early thirties; "Bulín" in their mid-forties; and "Toda una vida" in their mid-sixties.

Sexuality, its various manifestations or the repression of it, is an underlying motif of the characters' development. A striking feature of the four protagonists is their stereotypical construction: they are unabashedly male chauvinists for whom women are mere sexual objects: imposing mothers that castrate the lives of their sons; and wives who are in need of male domination or simply not worthy of men's consideration. Cerdín best exemplifies this attitude towards women when he concludes: "¡Yo no me caso! ¡Ni loco! Después de aguantar a la vieja (refiriéndose a la madre), no quiero saber nada de vivir con minas. Cuando tengo ganas, pago y chau. ¡Arrivederchi!" (34).

If such is the case, why does Torres Molina require that these characters be played by actresses who enter the stage dressed as women, change to male attire in front of the audience, and, before the curtain descends at the end of the play, return to their feminine dress? The play text reads: "Esta obra tiene como única condición para su representación, que los cuatro protagonistas deben ser representados por actrices" (11). Several partial explanations come to mind: the first and most obvious is the author's desire to deploy the theatrical mechanisms of dress substitution to call attention to the socially constructed nature of gender roles; that is, male and female are equally able to play social roles designated for the opposite sex: gendered behavior is not biologically determined. One can interpret the cross-dressing requisite as a mere role-playing technique that "performs" gender by having actresses performing male characters. This theory is further strengthened when one recalls that the exploration of role playing was a dramatic technique introduced in *Extraño juguete* as a mechanism to highlight the questioning of social codes.

The importance of distinct dress codes in the construction of gender differences is dramatized on stage before the first segment begins: "La obra comienza cuando una luz muy tenue ilumina a las 4 actrices que lentamente comienzan a *desvestirse* de mujeres y *vestirse* como chicos" (11; my emphasis). Showing on stage women in the act of "dressing up" as men underscores the contrived nature of "dressing up as women." The boys' conversation centers around the clothing and cosmetics necessary for the construction of the "feminine," alluding to the often painful rituals that accompany women's desire to fit traditional "feminine" beauty standards. El Inglés, for example, labels his sister's struggle to fit into smaller size jeans "Operación Bragueta":

> Mi hermana cada vez que se tiene que poner una lompa, llama a mi vieja . . . Y entre las dos se lo sube hasta la cintura. Después mi hermana se tira en la cama, respira hondo y ésa es la señal para que mi vieja se le tire encima y le suba el cierre. (14)

Aside from noting the difficulty of this task, the boys' comment on the discomfort produced by this sort of beauty ceremonial: "Che, miren tiene el pantalón tan ajustado que si respira hondo . . . ¡se queda en bolas!" (14). Pursuing unreasonable beauty standards frequently threatens life-sustaining human necessities—such as the ability to breathe freely.

The often violent consequences women must suffer by subscribing to these cultural fabrications are further highlighted by a discussion of women wearing high heels:

> Pajarito: (Mirando hacia la mujer imaginaria) Che miren, cómo hace equilibrio . . . no puede caminar con esos tacos finitos. (La imita).
> Cerdín: En cualquier momento ateriza.
> El Inglés: ¡Qué se jorobe! ¿Para qué los usa? (14)

Their conversation concludes with El Inglés' retelling of an incident involving El Flaco's sister: she was put in a plaster cast for two months after falling down while running after a bus in high heels. Wearing wigs and dyeing one's hair are among other constructions of the feminine evoked in this initial scene that calls attention to the many manifestations of this fabricated category.

The second scene treats "masculinity," the social expectations, cultural and physical, placed on young men. In a small Porteño bar, El Inglés, at seventeen, deliberates on how best to impress a young woman: "Me tendría que haber dejado los bigotes. Aparento más. Mañana voy a traer un libro de Borges, no mejor de Neruda, es más romántico . . . no, mejor de Borges, es más complicado. Más serio" (23). The pretense of serious intellectual inclinations and older, more mature looks are among young men's aspirations in order to seem more attractive to young women. Like women, men adhere to culturally fabricated notions of gender differences. While the social worth of young women is measured by their level of attractiveness to the opposite sex, young men's manhood is gauged by their success in conquering women.

What the actresses say while performing "male" characters typifies a misogynist ideology that highlights the objectification of women under patriarchy or, to recall Gambaro's words, in "ese mundo donde 'viven' las mujeres" (21).

In the first scene, machismo in its most graphic representation is staged as the four boys compare the size of their genitals to measure who is the most macho. From the very first segment, in adolescence, to the end of the play, in the characters' senior years, the desire for the sexual conquest of women is the center of gravity that holds this boys' club together. And while the play chronicles the characters' physical "maturity" into old age, their low regard for women, their lack of respect for them remains constant:

> Pajarito: ¿Vieron que hay más locas que locos?
> El Inglés: Y sí . . . yo leí en un libro, que las minas son mucho más idiotas que los hombres y por eso se vuelven locas más fácilmente.
> Pajarito: Parece que ya viene con una glándula de menos, o algo así.
> El Flaco: ¿Qué glándulas? Si no tienen glándulas . . . si vienen con la mitad de piezas de la fábrica . . . (19)

Significantly, this brief passage alludes to the "scientific" justifications that account for women's inferiority; El Inglés, after all, is founding his observation on knowledge attained in reading a "book." Such explanations, though articulated here by young boys, have been, at one point or another in history, advanced to establish the superiority of men. Similarly, this sort of ostensibly objective knowledge has been frequently used to justify the racial superiority of one group over others. By having actresses verbalize an extreme example of patriarchal chauvinism, Torres Molina demystifies male behavior and its natural superiority over women.

To further challenge patriarchal ideology, specifically Argentine chauvinism, Torres Molina appropriates a cultural form salient for its misogynist content and strong undercurrent of sadomasochist violence: the Argentine tango. Aside from alluding to the chronological passing of time, the titles of the play's segments evoke lyrics from popular tangos: "El metejón," "Toda una vida." Moreover, the dancing of tango dramatizes stylized copulation with a sense of pain-inducing dimensions of strong, acrobatic sexual pleasure (Foster, *Cultural* 38). The physically painful ramifications of this dance echo those that accompany beauty rituals, examples of constructions of the feminine that I discussed earlier. Torres Molina appropriates a typically misogynist expression of popular culture and parodies its meaning, which is similar to Josefina López's subversion of North American soap operas and Latin American "telenovelas." If one reads the playing of male characters by women as a literal performance of gender, one is inclined to read the use of tangos as fitting for the ideology of the play, but when one considers an alternative interpretation of the cross-gendered requisite, one appreciates the irony of this appropriation.

This second reading does not preclude the first one; rather, akin to similar techniques in Torres Molina's other works, . . . *Y a otra cosa mariposa* carries a dual level of signification. In this instance, a homoerotic subtext is encoded in the structural frame of the play. The cross-dressing requisite is a key element that forges the disruption of the heterosexual social codes. In fact, as Marjorie Garber has noted, the history of transvestism in Western culture intersects with the trajectory of homosexuality and gay identity; and although, as Garber notes, transvestism is not always consciously related to homosexuality, in certain cultural contexts, as in this Argentinean example, homosexuality might be viewed as the repressed that always returns (5-6).

The physical body on the stage is seen by some feminist and lesbian theorists as a potential site for challenging dominant—male, heterosexual—forms of representation. Jill Dolan writes:

> Sexual role-playing has implications for gender play: the way people perform sexuality influences how they wear their gender . . . A body displayed in representation that belongs to the female class is assumed to be heterosexual, since male desire organizes the representational system. (63)

The emphasis placed on the body in this play is noteworthy: the four male characters are not given names. Rather, their nicknames evoke their physical features: El Inglés, Cerdín, Flaco, and Pajarito. The last nickname strikes a dissonant chord: the character Pajarito is a homosexual in adult life, an occasional transvestite. Ironically, his nickname is the diminutive of "pájaro," which evokes phallocentrism in its most basic, graphic form—men's genitals. While Pajarito's coming out as a homosexual is initially received by his macho friends with displeasure, later in the play Pajarito's homosexual behavior is completely naturalized: on one occasion when the group meets to watch pornographic movies, Pajarito's dressing up for the event as a woman is no longer noticed by his friends. The play text reads: "Aparece Pajarito con el proyector. Se ha maquillado ojos y boca y está vestido de mujer, con tacos altos. Su aspecto de 'travestí'. Nadie parece notarlo" (49).

Homosexual innuendoes, such as the boys flirting with one another by playing "marica" roles, are evoked in the first part of the play and reappear in every segment thereafter. Recalling the social and cultural history of the tango is suggestive in this respect: David William Foster records that the tango originated in brothels, microcosms of masculine society at large, in which presumably clients and employees danced together, and he notes that something important has not been considered:

> But much has been made of the fact that the tango was foremost something men danced together in these houses. No social historian has explored whether this may be taken as one of homosexual motifs [sic] of Argentine culture that are still shrouded with almost impenetrable taboo—the male bonding of Gaucho culture and some other military traditions are other potential topics of interest here. (qtd. in *Cultural* 39-40)

Whatever the interpretation, the suggestion of homosexuality is possible; it is reiterated in the group's choice of pornographic movies, for example, which includes one dealing with lesbianism: "¿Cuál pasó primero?" asks Pajarito; El Inglés responds: "La de las dos minas . . . así vamos entrando en clima" (50).

In the play text, this disruption of gender categories, the questioning of knowledge and identity, is overdetermined by the verse of the poem that frames the play. Alejandra Pizarnik's poem reads: "y yo sola con mis voces, y vos, . . . tanto estás del otro lado que te confundo conmigo" (9). While the poetic voice is gendered, marked by the ending "sola," her addressee is left grammatically unmarked: it can be either a man or a woman. Whichever the case, the poetic voice identifies so closely with her addressee as to confuse it with herself, thus bringing to mind the crisis of a stable gendered identity.

The stereotypical male chauvinist discourse of the protagonists is acted out by women in men's garments, by women physically present; men's misogynist discourse constitutes the performance of a third category, the transvestite. Pajarito's figure unveils the power of transgressive desire: the staging of a woman, playing a homosexual man who dresses like a woman, is suggestive of a lesbian homoeroticism. Dolan writes: "disrupting the assumption of heterosexuality, and replacing male desire with lesbian desire . . . offers radical readings of the meanings produced by representation" (63). While the dramatic representation of a homosexual man is an open challenge to Argentina's particular set of repressive social values, the staging of lesbian women is still "unrepresentable." In order to represent lesbian homoeroticism, Torres Molina disguises it as a scandalous but socially more tolerable version of homosexuality—a man's. Whether male or female, both versions destabilize the patriarchal norms of heterosexuality and disrupt the dominant culture's system of representation. Furthermore, this type of dramatic strategy forces a realigning between the spectators and the performance that Dolan terms the "dynamics of desire." She writes: "When the locus of desire changes, the demonstration of sexuality and gender roles also changes . . ." (244). The change in desire challenges what de Lauretis notes as "the site in which social relations of gender and gender ideology is reproduced in everyday life" (17). In this manner, the presumed universal heterosexual contract that regulates dominant social conventions is challenged.

Pajarito's transvestism, it seems to me, functions precisely as the site in which the question of sexual desire crystallizes. Pajarito's sexual choice in his role as a man is that of other men: "¡No boludo! ¡Soy marica pero no mina! . . . Entendieron, hijos de . . . ¡Soy marica pero no mina!" (38). Since it is an actress who is playing the role of a male homosexual, the possibility of lesbian or bisexual desire is imposed. Dolan writes:

> The drag role requires the performer to quote the accepted conventions of gender behavior . . . By standing outside her gendered character, the performer makes gender available for discussion . . . When the role does not coincide with her biology, as it does when the lesbian plays a femme role, it is noncoincidental to the assumed heterosexuality of the representation of Woman . . . In the lesbian context, where the heterosexual assumption has been discarded, gender as representation gets detached from "the real" and becomes as plastic . . . The lesbian body, which articulates itself through female desire, stands already outside gender enculturation. (116-17)

Ironically, in the first segment of the play, the character of Pajarito is the one who comes closest to achieving sexual initiation and to proving his macho prowess. Later in the play, it is Pajarito who will distance himself from the perpetuation of the rituals of machismo.

This cross-dressing requisite functions as an ideological comment that brings to the surface the fact that all theatrical and gender assignments are, in a way, always ungrounded and contingent (Garber 39). From an epistemological perspective, this mechanism puts into question the idea of wholeness: of identity, self-sufficiency, self-knowledge. Garber notes that, "transvestism is a space of possibility structuring and confounding culture: the disruptive element that intervenes, not just a category crisis of male and female, but the crisis of category itself" (11).

It is worth noting that the performative techniques deployed in . . . *Y a otra cosa* resemble those that Torres Molina has utilized in her narrative. In "Impresiones de una futura mamá," one of the short stories from the collection *Dueña y señora,* a similar narrative strategy is used to tell of the romantic encounter between two women: Torres Molina appropriates the common boy-meets-girl formula and turns it into a dyke-meets-femme tale, a narration filled with pornographic detail that follows the "normal" descriptive formulas of heterosexual encounters. By normalizing homosexuality within the prevailing sexual codes, the author forges a deconstruction of heterosexuality and thus allows the presence of a competing homosexual discourse. Foster has rightly noticed this appropriation:

> Torres Molina's accommodation of the narrative pattern of heterosexual romance to nonchalant lesbian lovemaking is especially outrageous because, unlike the private worlds of the conventionalized forbidden and tragic homosexual lust, it does not posit a separate symbolic realm for the elaboration of the form of sexual coupling. Rather, it naturalizes that coupling by conveniently fitting it into a pre-existing erotic structure, thereby seeking to demonstrate that it is not substantively deviant from the sexual ethics of that structure. ("The Manipulation" 121-22)

While the desiring homosexual subject position is still only a subtext in the dramatic performance, the narrative text treats openly the representation of lesbian desire. In fact, *Dueña y señora* is the first collection of explicitly lesbian writing in Latin America (Foster, *Gay* 131).

Aside from constituting an open challenge to a particular set of repressive social values, especially in regards to lesbianism, *Dueña y señora* tested Argentina's nascent redemocratization process. Argentine writer and psychotherapist Martha Berlin notes in the prologue to the 1983 edition:

> No soy ingenua respecto al impacto de este libro en el Buenos Aires femenino y masculino, en esta primavera del ochenta y tres, en la alborada de un proceso de democratización para nuestro país. Sólo al

> precio de la verdad podremos adquirir la amplitud de consciencia para el ejercicio de sus funciones sociales si la palabra sobre su sexo sigue callada . . . Un nuevo universo femenino-masculino es el encargado de abrir las prisiones mentales que son el oprobio de la humanidad. Susana sabe que escribió un texto dilemático, porque no permite enfrentarlo con ambivalencia, en el texto y en el subtexto transita una clarísima ideología. (5-9)

In order to forge a lesbian subject position for the stage, the author, while subverting the dominant heterosexual codes, remains within the parameters of the permissible for Argentine theater audiences.[4] For comparative purposes, it is worth recalling that during the same period in Mexico City Jesusa Rodríguez's lesbian theater, El Hábito, known to have nude performances, managed, if with difficulty, to circumvent government regulations and to gain the respect of some sectors of the Mexican cultural elite. In the Argentine context, Torres Molina avails herself of the theatrical mechanisms of substitution to frame the homoerotic subtext.

The title of the play is another indication of its underlying ideology: "Y a otra cosa mariposa" brings to mind, among other things, the colloquial manner of evoking the casual passing from one facet to another: it alludes to the metamorphosis undergone by the characters throughout the play—the cycle of life. By returning the male characters to their initial adolescent stage and by having the actresses return to their feminine dress before the curtain is dropped, . . . *Y a otra cosa mariposa* intimates the all-encompassing nature of life, while it also emphasizes the inescapable sexual and gendered feature of the human condition.

The circularity of life is further highlighted by the dramatic space of the first and last scenes: the play ends in the same plaza where the first scene is staged. The four old men, now in their mid-sixties, sit on a bench discussing ways to deter their human decay. In distinction to the first scene, where the boys' dialogue centers on the rituals that accompany the artificial constructs that mark gender differences, on this occasion the old men's conversation focuses on basic human survival—how to maximize the preservation of human life. Dieting and exercise are evoked not as ways to attaining beauty and sexual enhancement but as mechanisms to preserve the body. Not surprisingly, the play ends with the boys' celebration of the objectification of women via pornography: "¡Si las minas están para eso!" (56), El Pajarito and El Inglés intone.

In addition, the title . . . *Y a otra cosa mariposa* alludes to the passing from heterosexuality to homosexuality, for "mariposa," like "pajarito," is a colloquial expression that designates homosexuals— yet another insouciant denaturalization of homosexuality. As I have been demonstrating in this section, the theatrical devices of . . . *Y a otra cosa mariposa* process homosexual desire and denaturalize it. The transvestite component creates a theatrical dislocation that destabilizes gender categories and insinuates the power of transgressive desire: homoeroticism. In fitting the gay invocation into preexisting structures, Torres Molina's text seeks to suggest that homosexuality is not an aberration of heterosexuality.

Torres Molina in her critique of Argentine machismo yields space for other forms of desire not operating within patriarchal expectations of heterosexuality while still inhabiting Griselda Gambaro's "mundo donde 'viven' las mujeres" (21). By contrast, as we shall see in the next chapter, Carmen Boullosa, writing in Mexico, ventures into the fabrication of a world in which patriarchy ceases to dictate the norms, a universe solely created for and inhabited by women: a society of witches.

Chapter 3: On Dramatic Bodies, Witches, and Feminine Dramaturgy

> Debe haber otro modo . . .
> Otro modo de ser humano y libre
> Otro modo de ser.
> (Castellanos, *Mujer* 7)

Mexican Women Playwrights, and their Contexts: Colonial to Contemporary Feminisms

Unlike the other countries discussed in this study, Mexico holds a more abundant tradition of women playwrights. The Colonial period, as mentioned in the introduction, attested to the extraordinary genius of the Americas' first woman playwright, Sor Juana Inés de la Cruz. Through Leonor, one of the characters of *Los empeños de una casa,* Sor Juana voices her passion for learning, lamenting the constraints society placed on women's intellectual development, a theme she later developed in her celebrated autobiographical letter "Respuesta a Sor Filotea." Specialists in Colonial literature find particularly remarkable in Sor Juana's writing her clear awareness of her decision to depart from the norm of her epoch and her courageous confrontation with the consequences of those choices (Bergmann 152).

As a prodigy poet, thinker, and a defender of women's right to pursue an intellectual life, Sor Juana has been a source of inspiration and a role model for other women writers of the Americas. As in the English tradition, where Virgina Woolf in *A Room of One's Own* remarked on the first Englishwoman to support herself by her writing, the seventeenth-century playwright Aphra Behn, "here begins the freedom of the mind . . . for now that Aphra Behn had done it, girls could say 'I can make money by my pen'" (67). In the Hispanic world, Sor Juana is frequently recognized as being the first woman on this continent to initiate the struggle for women's intellectual independence. Rosario Castellanos in *Mujer que sabe latín,* for example, begins with Sor Juana a list of women whom she views as role models because they chose to be true to themselves despite societal restrictions. She writes: "Para elegirse a sí misma y preferirse por encima de los demás se necesita haber llegado a una situación límite. Situación límite por su intensidad, dramatismo, su desgarradora intensidad física" (*Mujer* 19-20). The exemplary life of this striking nun has been revisited by contemporary dramatists, critics, and film directors. Among the U.S. Latina playwrights, Estela Portillo-Trambley, for example, in her play *Sor Juana* recovers the Hispanic tradition, more specifically the Mexican cultural heritage, thus connecting the Anglo American and Latin American cultural spectrums which the U.S. Latino case study, discussed in the next chapter, dramatizes so well.

For the comparative nature of this project, it is worth noticing that, unlike the Brazilian and, to a lesser extent, the Argentine and U.S. Latino cases, Mexican drama has been well researched and taught at some universities where North American scholars of Latin American theater are located. While in Brazil the late 1960s and early 1970s evidenced an increased production of a body of literary and dramatic work written by women, during that same period Mexico had an even greater number of women writers. Among the dramatists, Luisa Josefina Hernández, Maruxa Villalta, Elena Garro, and Rosario Castellanos received recognition within the literary and theatrical establishment. Of this group, the work of Hernández y Villalta seems reactionary when compared with their two other counterparts. For example, Luisa Josefina Hernández in a 1991 interview, when asked to comment on the presence of women on the Mexican stage, remarks the following: ". . . Occure que realmente es notable la exigua cantidad de mujeres que escriben para el teatro . . . En primer lugar las que hay no son muy conocidas, otras no son muy buenas aunque sean conocidas" (Andrade 199). Hernández's comment is, among other things, intriguing because it inadvertently omits the experimental work of Castellanos and of her contemporaries: Sabina Berman and Carmen Boullosa, two Mexican playwrights who have been very prolific during the last two decades. As with Brazil, most of the plays written by members of the generation of Luisa Josefina Hernndez lie within the parameters of a theatrical form that some feminist dramatic theorists consider reactionary and contrary to radical feminist goals. Yet, as Assunção's *Lua nua* demonstrates, plays written in the realist form do not necessarily preclude the theatricalization of a feminist ideology. Moreover, one might recall that fabricating strong female characters as subjects of a text and, for once, creating a position of spectatorship for women is a relatively recent phenomenon given the historical exclusion women writers have experienced in U.S. Latino, Latin American, North American, and European theaters.

Salient on the Mexican stage for its pioneering experimentation with dramatic forms and for its staunch feminist stance is a 1976 play by Rosario Castellanos, *El eterno femenino.* This piece critiques the social predicament of middle-class Mexican women by debunking cultural myths that have historically circumscribed their lives. In line with the tradition in contemporary Mexican theater that dramatizes historical revisions, *El eterno femenino* stages women, among others, La Malinche, Eve, Sor Juana, Josefa Ortiz de Domínguez, Carlota de Maximiliano, and Adelita, and has them recounting their versions of their historical lives, that is, from a woman's perspective. As in Josefina López's *Simply María,* *El eterno femenino* highlights family, religion, and national history as they conspire to indoctrinate Mexican women into believing that their only options in life are those handed down to them by patriarchy.[1] On the significance of *El eterno femenino,* Kirsten F. Negro notes:

> *The Eternal Feminine* can be considered a liminal text, a threshold between plays written by women about women's problems, mostly in a realistic manner, to "show how things are," to ones that dissect the institutions and social practices that "make these things the way they are," including their chosen medium, the theatre, This is a fundamental move that allows for plays that . . . open up spaces where women can position themselves as agents of action and radical change (138).

In *El eterno femenino,* Castellanos dramatizes an ideology that permeates her writing in other genres and stages the critical presence of an experimental, feminist dramatic body in contemporary Mexican theater.

Critics, among them Jean Franco, have pointed out that contemporary Mexican women are engaged in a struggle for a presence in the public domain of Mexican society and for the power to participate in the interpretative sphere. While one cannot ignore that some Mexican women are attaining visibility and the power to represent, one needs to recognize that these women constitute a very small, elite group. As a point of fact, the majority of the female protagonists in the works of Mexican women authors are from the upper middle class. Although it is a broad phenomenon everywhere in the arts, which by their nature are about and geared to the educated classes because they are produced by them, one ought to acknowledge that the absence of women writers from economically and racially disadvantaged backgrounds in Mexico is similar to the Argentinean and the Brazilian examples included in this study. An author with the type of socioeconomic background of U.S. Latina Josefina López is very unlikely in Mexican society: Chicana writers, like other North American women of color, are in a category of their own. When working-class women have appeared in Mexican literature, they have done so through the mediation of a writer who does not belong to that group, as with Jesusa Palancares in Elena Poniatowka's *Hasta no verte Jesús mío.* And as in the United States, in Mexico class is intertwined with race. While most of the Mexican population is composed of "mestizos," the offspring of Indians and Spanish, those closer to European racial models are invariably at the center of cultural, political, and economic power.

For the comparative nature of this project, another anecdote worth citing involves the Mexican-American essayist Richard Rodriguez. While on a business trip to Mexico City with the intention of finding a publisher for a translation of his latest book, *Days of Obligation: Conversations with my Mexican Father* (1993), the very dark-skinned, indigenous-looking Rodriguez was confronted by the director of one publishing house who looked at him scrupulously and explained, "Well, I don't know, Richard, I don't know. Here we don't have writers who look like you do" (Rodriguez). Elena Urrutia, the director of the women's studies program at El Colegio de México, further assesses the interface between race, class, and women writers in comtemporary Mexico as she observes:

> No hay todavía una escritora de extracción popular campesina, obrera, ni mucho menos. Es evidente, para ser escritora en México necesitas tener un bagaje cultural determinado. No necesariamente que hayas hecho un doctorado pero te hayas inmerso en una cultura, una sensibilidad determinada y eso supone en México, un nivel sociocultural determinado. (qtd. in Costantino 28)

Unlike Argentina and Brazil, countries that have lived under military dictatorships that fostered periods of legal censorship in all forms of cultural productions, Mexico suffered a more subtle suppression: the regulation of the country's morality and the government's ability to maintain its power are executed by silencing its critics. Examples are the 1991 dismissals of the journalist Manu Dornbierer and the actor Héctor Suárez. Dornbierer's overtly critical journalism led to his discharge from the newspaper *El Excelsior.* Televisa, the independent television network that maintains close ties with the Mexican government, functioning often as its auxiliary, fired

Suárez for trespassing the limits of what is permissible. With the approval of the government, the centralized Catholic church has gradually exerted the authority to promulgate a particularly reactionary brand of morality, an ideology that strongly affects the lives of women. Among the most obvious issues are abortion and birth control. Thus, to ensure the victory of a right-wing party that would maintain the illegal status of abortion and would protect Catholic morality, the Mexican bishops in 1991 issued a statement declaring that it was sinful not to vote in political elections (Franco, *A Touch* 48).

Spurred by the desire to continually disrupt staid Mexican society, the dramatic performances of lesbian writer, performer, and cabaret owner Jesusa Rodríguez often include satirical attacks on some of the most sacred icons of Mexican nationalism, such as the Virgin of Guadalupe and, in some instances, current politicians. Rodríguez's theater has survived despite the many government attempts to close the premises by, for example, not renewing the required commercial licenses. Without specifically censuring an establishment owned, run, and frequented by homosexuals, the government's unofficial policy is to make it difficult to stay in business. In an interview Jesusa Rodríguez states:

> I believe that here in Mexico it is more a matter of self-censorship than censorship. You actually realize that unless you censor yourself you are not going to please and they will put pressure on you. Also, there is a fear of taking risks, of risking one's economic position. I have observed that fundamentally people are more afraid of doing something, of taking risks and seeing what happens . . . I have no desire to censor myself at all, and cannot. However, what I would like to stress is that there is a path that is not taken out of fear . . . (Franco, A Touch 53)

By engaging in this discussion, I simply intend to highlight some aspects of a complex sociocultural context in which a less visible but equally oppressive power prevails, a ponderous patriarchal ideology that continues to influence the positions Mexican women assume in public.

In the 1980s, partly because of an increase in commercial interest in women's writing, the publication of Mexican women authors doubled in number, creating what has been viewed in Mexican literary circles as a "boom" of feminine writing. The frequently recognized women authors include, Julieta Campos, Carmen Boullosa, Sabina Berman, Cristina Pacheco, Laura Esquivel, Jesusa Rodriguez, Sara

Sefchovich, Margo Glantz, Guadalupe Loaeza and Angeles Mastreta, winner of the 1997 Romulo Gallegos literary prize. Aside from performance artist Jesusa Rodriguez, Sabina Berman and Carmen Boullosa are the most prolific playwrights. The dramatic production of Boullosa and Berman continues the experimentation with dramatic form and exploration of gender constructions initiated on the contemporary Mexican stage by Castellanos' *El eterno femenino*.[2]

Like Leilah Assunção in Brazil, many contemporary Mexican writers refute associations with the ideological concerns that accompany a feminist position. Carmen Boullosa is a Mexican author who, like Assunção, rejects any attempts to associate her with political movements (that is, feminism) or with a generation of Mexican writers. Yet, not denying that her condition as a woman affects her writing, Boullosa remarks: "La 'literatura de mujeres' es una de tantas modas y éstas no son para que se les juzgue. Está bien que existan, pero me irrita estar en una moda. [. . .] Me pienso escritor, no escritora" (qtd. in Costantino 172-74). Although in public interviews Boullosa rejects political affinity with feminist concerns, her artistic work embodies feminist strains.

Other Worlds, Other Stages: Feminine Dramaturgy

> Vete solo papá, ¡vete! . . . Por fin podré ser lo que la noche obliga.
> (Boullosa, Cocinar 82)

Carmen Boullosa's work appears in all the circles of the Mexican literary and artistic world, among the establishment as well as the margins in Jesusa Rodríguez's lesbian cabaret-bar. Over the last two decades, Boullosa and Rodríguez have worked together in many cooperative productions in Rodríguez's El Hábito, which many consider the site of today's Mexican avant-garde. At times it seems as if Boullosa's remarkable work in the theater, particularly the one done during the 1970s and 1980s, is overshadowed by her more recent and abundant narrative production. With seven novels to her credit and translations of her work into several languages, Boullosa has captured an audience in the U.S. and Europe. Given the critical acclaim Boullosa's work has received abroad, it was fitting that she was the winner of the 1997 Anna-Seghers-Foundation award in literature, an award presented by Germany's Academy of Fine Arts. While "heretic," "fantastic," "experimental" are adjectives critics, in Mexico and abroad, frequently use to characterize Boullosa's artistic production, gender-specific issues like the exploration of female identity and its representation in theater and literature are a recurring concern in Boullosa's work and are particularly salient in the three pieces that comprise *Teatro herético.* Departing from a social realist form, as deployed by Leilah Assunção's in *Lua nua,* Carmen Boullosa, like Susana Torres Molina, opts for an experimental form. But whereas Susana Torres Molina's playtext still relies on certain Aristotelian features, such as the plot's chronology, for example, Carmen Boullosa's experimentation with the dramatic medium is of a different orientation.

Cocinar hombres, one of the plays in the collection, is a dramatic text that gives strong evidence of characteristics associated with feminine dramaturgy. The feminist ideology incarnated in the play is manifested through the issue it stages: women's desire, women's sexuality, the vindication of a type of woman that tradition has deemed evil (for example, witches), and the flight to a world beyond patriarchy. The use of stage space and of dramatic time departs radically from conventional dramatic forms. These disruptions of patriarchal theatrical models prompt the discussion of *Cocinar hombres* as a play representative of a feminine dramaturgy. As with the question of *l'écriture féminine,* the possibility of "feminine dramaturgy" remains a debated topic among North American and European feminist theater circles. And while a few Latin Americans, among them Luisa Valenzuela and Nelly Richard, have theorized about the subversive quality of language in the writing of some Latin American women, the question of an essentially feminine dramaturgy has not been addressed in discussions of Latin American theater.

Coincidentally, in "Mis brujas favoritas," Luisa Valenzuela theorizes about a much debated aspect of women's writing and feminist criticism—a form of writing that by its specific use of language distinguishes itself as a product of a woman writer, as "feminine writing." Valenzuela broaches this question through "aquello en lo que no se cree—o quisiera no creerse o no se pudiera creer—pero que las hay, las hay . . ." (88). For Valenzuela, women writers who disturb preestablished discursive modes are like modern-day witches, contemporaries of those women who were forced into silence. Bonfires buried the voices of witches; later asylums concealed the outcries of the so-called hysterics. In agreement with French proponents of *l'écriture féminine,* Valenzuela believes that the subversive quality of women's writing originates in the writer's connection to her own biologically determined feminine functions. *L'écriture féminine* focuses its debate on language and maintains that biologically based differences in female sexuality rise to a form of female textuality that can subvert male signification. Writing with the body allows for an excessive flow of blood, birth, and sexual metaphors in a nonlinear, florid, stream-of-consciousness style that inscribes sexual differences as the content and form of cultural feminist expression. *L'écriture féminine,* as it theorizes the stage space, harkens back to Artaud's theater of cruelty, which overturns the authority of the text to privilege the body and gesture as the primordial theatrical essence. Cixous' dramatic model suggests that if the stage is woman, plots will no longer be necessary: "A single gesture is enough, but one that can transform the world" (Dolan 8). The play examined in this section, *Cocinar hombres* lacks an Aristotelian plot; instead, it consists of dialogue in which the two protagonists participate equally in their roles of speaker and listener; through this medium, the characters act out their concerns which will function in the play as a problem-solving technique that will later allow them to make empowering decisions.

Cocinar hombres is an experimental play divided into a dream sequence and two acts that stage two young women's rites of initiation into a world inhabited only by women, a society of witches. The nonmimetic nature of the play is established in the preface where the author sets forth the background for the play's dramatic action: two women awake from their sleep to discover the transformation of their bodies from preadolescence to mature womanhood. The metamorphosis derives from their previous night's initiation into a circle which the author describes as

> . . . más restringido—o más amplio, si hemos de creer a aquellos autores que aseguran que hubo un tiempo en el cual las lamias volando protegidas por la noche cometiendo cuantos horrores podían, constituían la tercera parte de la población de Francia— La autora pide disculpas si la cualidad de brujas de estos dos personajes excede o trastoca las definiciones de la tradición popular. (46)

By describing the dramatic space as "more open or more restricted," according to who tells the story, the playwright sets the stage for possibilities that surpass the norm, that is, she intentionally and ironically fails to establish definite positions. Moreover, Boullosa playfully highlights the authorial power that inheres in the telling of stories that later might come to constitute popular "truths." The author

Dramatic Bodies and Feminine Dramaturgy 65

implicitly challenges all previous constructions of the real and of the surreal; she provokes transformations that defy established norms. Writers have the power, Boullosa reminds us, to fabricate definitions that are later integrated into the sphere of traditional culture. The gender inflection evoked between "autores" and "autora" recalls that historically men have held the monopoly on the construction of stories, of history, of myths, of knowledge. By inserting itself into the authorial discourse, Boullosa's gender, "la autora," disrupts this tradition. She further transforms patriarchal concepts and images of witches by presenting them as strong, likeable characters who, contrary to mythical constructs, do not terrorize and steal children: a symbolic feminist gesture that recovers patriarchy's evil women.

The dream sequence that opens the play finds the two girls, Ufe and Wine, recalling their kidnapping by the witches, an action which sets off the transformation of their ten-year-old bodies into those of twenty-three-year-old women. Contrary to Western paradigm which views the number thirteen as ominous, in this play, the elapsing of thirteen years will mark the beginning of a new life, a new world for the protagonists. This initial framing scene dramatizes the startling experience of suddenly being looked at differently, as a woman. Ufe recalls:

> Detuve el coche en la cuneta, y cuando me bajé había muchas personas mirándome y supe que yo tenía el cuerpo de mi mamá. Yo ya no era yo, y todos lo que estaban ahí se daban cuenta. Yo ya no tenía mi cuerpo: tenía el cuerpo de mi mamá . . . (48)

While the gender of the observers is not determined in this passage, the allusion to the male gaze, the patriarchal construction of "women's lookedness" that film theorist Laura Mulvey has articulated elsewhere, is implicitly evoked. This passage alludes to the process of gender identification that begins with the body: through her body woman is identified as object/woman. With regards to the theatrical performance, the body presented as a topic for exploration calls attention to the visual aspect of the body in representation and in social codes which place it at the center of gender identification and of other theories which develop subject positions based on biological differences.

Cocinar hombres introduces characters who openly discuss issues related to the experience of being a woman in a patriarchal society; it presents women's bodies, and women's relationships to their bodies, as central concerns seen from a feminist perspective. In this case, women are no longer the stage upon which men project their fantasies. Ufe and Wine like their bodies, their desires, their friendships; together they discover options outside of dominant discourses and desires. Through Ufe the play stages the complicity of women in their own objectification within the confines of patriarchy; it represents a character who does not question the cultural impositions placed upon her. Alternatives in identities and desires are introduced through the play's other character, Wine.

For Ufe and Wine knowledge, what they understand and feel, is achieved through their physical body; "lo que sientes en el cuerpo," "hasta olía yo distinto," "Me pesaba distinto la cabeza" (51-52) are conceits that underscore the centrality of their body to their identity, to their experience of themselves. Significantly, Ufe remembers traditional norms, and those perceptions continue to regulate her experience. By contrast, Wine is free from those standards and, consequently, she is able to interpret her body from a different perspective. She affirms: "Yo no me acuerdo de mi escuela porque no me acuerdo de nada. No tengo memoria" (52). Her lack of memory presents the spectator with another world, a world of the night and of pleasure, free from any sort of societal restriction. The play performs the appropriation of women's bodies for themselves through the presentation of breasts as a topic of conversation. In patriarchal imagery breasts are fetishistic concepts ("adornos") for the pleasure and excitement of men: "Por lo menos por teléfono no te clavaría la vista en los que llamas adornos" (61), whereas in the new context breasts nurture women's pleasures, including those derived specifically from a biologically "feminine" body: "Yo siempre quise tener mi cuerpo de mujer . . . y pensaba, ¿cómo serán mis pechos? ¿cómo se sentirán? Nunca toqué ningunos de niña" (61). The two women help each other to appreciate their bodies and to develop positive ways in which to accept them.

In addition to breasts, shoes, another fetishistic image, are deconstructed in *Cocinar hombres*. The sexual connotation that traditionally accompanies women's shoes is subverted when shoes are introduced with the important function of holding Ufe and Wine to the ground while they are deciding whether to join the society of witches or stay on earth. Noteworthy in this respect is that shoes cover women's feet, a site with feminine subversive potential, according to the theoretical postulations of Luisa Valenzuela. If Ufe and Wine take off their shoes, they expose their feet, they set them free and liberate themselves from patriarchal order and fly away to another world.

From a feminist perspective, the recovery of women's bodies necessitates the acknowledgement of women's desire and diverse expressions of sexuality. Incapable of recalling her past, Wine defines her memory in terms of what she desires: "Sé lo que siempre he querido; lo que siempre he deseado eso sí, pero recuerdos ninguno" (51). Rather than monolithic compulsory heterosexuality, which enforces heterosexuality as "natural" for all women, Boullosa challenges this notion by presenting multiple desiring subject positions (98): lesbian desire ("lo que hicimos fue jalonearnos y darnos de pellizcos" [64]) and masturbation ("en el sexo otro oprimiéndote y esas manos no fueran de nadie ni pudieran serlo y no pusieras tus manos en donde pudieras darte gusto" [52]). Furthermore, Boullosa stages another major taboo in patriarchal Mexican literature: sexual desire during pregnancy[3]: "¿Qué tengo ganas de tacos? No . . . Tengo ganas todo el tiempo, con un hombre se entiende" (70). Everything is permissible in a world beyond the confinements of patriarchy. Wine states: "Aquí nadie te va a reclamar si amas a un hombre y a un hijo" (67). In distinction to the Argentine example, where homosexuality is framed within heterosexual codes, here lesbian desire is represented for what it is—women's desire for other women.

In order to investigate her desire for motherhood and the traditional family, in Act II, Ufe cooks up several men. In this scene the spectator is confronted with the fact that women are the ones who bear men: women cook-up-create men on their own. Heretical disobedience is underscored by presenting women as capable of creation and production without the help or consent of men, similar to the way God/Gods create men in patriarchal religions:

> Wine: . . . Cocínate un hombre . . . Cocínatelo y vete con él.
> Ufe: Un hombre para desearlo; a mi gusto, a mi medida, hecho para lo que yo quiera . . .
> Wine: A la medida de tu deseo . . . (68)

Breaking away from the prescribed roles satirized in Castellanos' *El eterno femenino,* Ufe and Wine are active subject producers of meaning and men. Reversing patriarchy, *Cocinar hombres* stages women's creation of men, made to the measure of their desire and imagination.

Motherhood, an important female identity mark, is also explored from a woman's perspective here. Once again, Boullosa introduces various options available to women. Ufe, for example, represents the traditionally prescribed role; she wants children and speaks in defense of motherhood: "cuando pienso en arrullar a mi hijo . . . lo que convierte la maternidad en una gran pasió . . . los niños son como la cara del triperio que tenemos dentro" (66). Wine, not desiring children, fears the consequences of what patriarchy promotes about women who do not experience motherhood: without children a woman is "vieja," "estéril," "seca," "inútil" (67).

Similar to Milcha Sánchez-Scott's play *Latina,* role-playing in this drama is a problem-solving technique, which avails women with the opportunity to build community among them. The two characters engage in a to-have-or-not-to-have-a-baby act: Ufe plays a pregnant wife and Wine acts the role of the friend and confidant. Through their role-playing, Wine supports the fantasies of Ufe; jointly, they look at the pros and cons of having a baby. Wine reminds Ufe that there are alternatives to marriage and having children. The final decision, however, is still Ufe's individual choice.

In addition to celebrating community among women, Boullosa vindicates witches who are traditionally rendered as hideous, silent, and monstrous through myth and narrative because they represent female power and sexuality. *Cocinar hombres* subverts this tradition by portraying witches in a new light, strong and likable precisely because they embody female power and sexuality. Boullosa introduces witches and the supernatural to present a dimension uncontrolled by men.

Along with the subversion of myths and other traditional constructions of women's bodies, desires, and sexuality, Boullosa deploys experimental techniques that deviate from patriarchal dramatic forms. Significant in *Cocinar hombres* is its lack of particular indications of spatial arrangements.[4] The only directions given in the text are those that situate Wine and Ufe in a house without windows and doors. Furthermore, if these protagonists' remove their shoes, they will float away. Hence, the play creates a sense of flotation, of a nonstatic world. A careful examination at the protagonists names further underscore the sense of movement: In changing the order of the words that compose Ufe's name, one finds the word "fue," the past tense of the verb "to be" and "go"; whereas the name Wine, when pronounced in Spanish, mimics the sound of the word "vine," the past tense of the verb to come. Ufe/Fue's character represents the past; her name underscore the action of leaving behind man's world. Wine/Vine symbolizes the arriving of the new world, the witches' world. In contrast to realist dramatic spatial arrangements, this play constructs otherworldly spaces, supernatural worlds.

As with the play's spatial arrangements, the dramatic chronology is also disturbed. The introduction reads:

> Ambas al acostarse tenían 10 años y al despertar tienen 23, no por haber dormido el tiempo equivalente a su crecimiento sino por haber sido llevadas a una ceremonia ... (46)

The rest of the play takes place in one night, the time given to Ufe and Wine to decide whether they want to join the society of witches or return to earth. But even that night is constantly infiltrated with references to other chronologies: reminiscences of Ufe's and Wine's youth, future possibilities, historical time. During the ceremony of the witches, Ufe remembers:

> Ufe: Olía a carne quemada, a carne de mujer cocinada ... Cualquier día nos va a tocar a ti y a mí, nos van a cocinar poniendo el fuego en nuestros riñones ... que me quemen viva ... me martiricen, me claven la marca de bruja. (57)

Ufe rightly fears the same will happen to them. By invoking the historical period of the Inquisition's burning of witches, Boullosa reminds the protagonists and the spectators of earlier efforts to eradicate those who did not adhere to patriarchal norms. The consequences are disturbing, to say the least.

The play ends with a renunciation of all previous desires and the entrance into another world through the creation of a new language, another characteristic of "feminine language and dramaturgy." Coincidentally, much discussion today on "feminine language and feminine writing" centers on the metaphor of cooking by women. Some writers and feminist critics have come to view the domestic domain of the kitchen, historically reserved for women, as the site for subverting that feminine space by engaging in the biblicaly defined masculine act of creation, of writing.[5] *Como agua para chocolate* by another contemporary Mexican writer, Laura Esquivel, is an obvious example; in *Cocinar hombres* Boullosa takes to the stage the metaphor of cooking to represent a feminist reproduction of men, language, and dramaturgy.

Striking a blow against patriarchy, Ufe and Wine opt for a world of night where women control the dreams of men: "Luego vas a visitar las camas de los hombres para sembrarles deseos y encontrarás el infinito orgullo de ser lo que eres" (68). The protagonists describe their new world as a place "donde no viven los hombres . . ." but where they will hear "los secretos de las hojas de los árboles, los secretos del viento, el sonido de las bisagras de las almas de los hombres, el sonido de tus deseos cuando caen o cuando brotan . . ." (69). It is interesting to note the allusions in this passage to mother earth, to nature. Boullosa's description of a uniquely woman's space coincides with the return to mother earth and nature, which, again, is a position congenial to the essentially "natural" specificities of women's bodily functions and "feminine writing." Yet a counterargument exists: In this strict sense of the Cartesian paradigm, the allusion to nature has been associated with women precisely because they are uncontrollable in temperament. Reason and intellectual endeavors are implicitly the exclusive domains of men. Under this framework, the binary oppositional paradigm remains unchallenged.

Women's power reigns in the society of witches. Women's bodies, their desires, and their ability to reproduce without men are a source of empowerment. In the last episode Ufe finally decides: "vete solo papá, ¡vete!, llévate contigo el cariño, la confianza, el odio . . . la envidia, váyanse, váyanse: por fin podré ser lo que la noche obliga" (82). The law of the Father will no longer be pertinent to their lives. Wine explains that in their new world they will name themselves and will have the ability to change their names on a daily basis: "cada día llamarse con otro nombre es tener todos los nombres del mundo" (68). In embracing all possible names, they first recover those silenced for going against patriarchy:

> Primero, todos los nombres de las nuestras: Noctiluca, Herodiade, Holda, Diana, Abundia, Bensozia, Títuba, Abigail, y luego las que vivieron entre los hombres: Catalina, a quien acosaron, hicieron efecto de una intriga y luego encerraron . . . cuando veían que ya iba a morir, la sacaban para prolongar su tortura, por igual motivo la quemaron con madera fresca; Magdalena, que enloqueció y fue perseguida porque querían arrancarle el alma . . . (69)

The entrance into this other world is determined by the protagonists' erasure of any recollections from their lives on earth: "¡Ya no recuerdo nada!" (82). The final words said on stage are the language of the new society. In unison Ufe and Wine recite: "Oviv ojih le odanew le oíroma le ogeuj le se eliab etse adilas al adapacse al atreup al se ehcon atse . . ."

(82). The readers and spectators of the play are confronted with a language in reverse of patriarchal linguistic codes.

As in the two other plays that constitute the collection *Teatro herético, Alba y las once mil vírgenes* and *Propusieron a María,* in *Cocinar hombres* Boullosa follows the definition of "herejía" : "Error en materia de fe, sostenido con pertinacia . . . sentencia errónea contra una ciencia o arte . . . Palabra injuriosa . . . Opinión no aceptada por la autoridad establecida" (*Diccionario Pequeño Larousse* 1986). By disrupting deep-rooted patriarchal ideology, Boullosa deconstructs discourses of the church, art, and science. Like *Simply María,* which is discussed in the next chapter, *Cocinar hombres* questions the creation of gender roles; yet, *Cocinar* goes a step further by proposing that women are capable of reproduction without the consent or aid of men: Women construct a world, a language (a dramaturgy?) of their own.

As to the question of "feminine dramaturgy" and of *Cocinar hombres*' pertinence to this orientation, the play's thematic and formal expression demonstrates the extent to which it deviates from patriarchal norms. Yet, one must also address the issue of essentialism from which feminine dramaturgy draws its premises: this Mexican example, like the Argentine case, rests on gender notions of "woman" as a universal sign. In this respect, their particular contexts fail to account for significant differences between them and their European and North American counterparts. Why search for specificities in Latin American, in this case Mexican, women's writing when, aside from the particular cultural references, they do not exist?

Sue-Ellen Case has rightly observed the limitations of feminine dramaturgy: it fails to account for variations in race, class, and culture among women. All the difference is framed in terms of the sameness defined by women's separation from men (Dolan 8-9). In the formation of Woman as a transcendent, universal subject position, cultural feminism and *l'écriture féminine* erect a new monolith from which it becomes difficult to diverge (Dolan 9). Accordingly, in regards to the Mexican context from which *Cocinar hombres* emerges, one must ask which "Mexican" is represented in this play and who is the receiver of these representations.

From a feminist materialist position, one that insistently views feminism as a social movement and not just as a literary methodology, issues of race and class are not to be ignored. As I mentioned earlier, Mexico and, to a lesser degree, Argentina are countries that, like the United States and Brazil, are racially and economically stratified. In light of this reality, one is compelled to ask how can racially and economically disadvantaged women, those who lack interpretative power, enter the world of reproducing meaning, knowledge, and power? How effective is it for materialist feminist aims to abandon everything, including life and the plight of women in the here and now? The question remains.

CHAPTER 4: STAGING DIFFERENCE: PERFORMING BORDER IDENTITIES

> Mexico is in my blood . . . And America is in my heart . . . (López, *Simply* 141)

U.S. Latino Theater and Its Contexts

Like their Spanish and Portuguese counterparts in the Southern hemisphere, the first theatrical events in North American territory date back to the seventeenth century; they were Christian plays performed in Spanish. While these dramatic performances bear testimony to the existence of Spanish-speaking people in the United States, some of them of European extraction, it is misleading to associate with these representations the connotations of the current terms "Chicano" or "Latino." The audiences attending these pioneering dramatic pieces did not write or produce them. Their living experience on North American soil was not a thematic basis for these scripts. Instead, the significance of these early performances lies in their attestation to populations and cultures that inhabited this territory before the arrival of the English settlers. Still, because the construction of what constitutes "North American" has been, until very recently, unquestionably centered on the white, English-speaking, European constituencies, other nonwhite cultures and languages coexisting in the same land have been slighted, with the result that a partial, deceptive, and Eurocentric view of North American history and culture emerges.[1]

In academic discussions centered on American culture and history, the acknowledgement of non-European cultures is the offspring of a relatively recent social phenomenon. In the late 1960s, civil rights movements of American minorities sharing a history of exclusion and racial discrimination, demanded basic human rights. Pressured by this political activism, college and university campuses began to recruit people of color more consistently. Once in the university settings, African-Americans, Native-Americans, Asian-Americans, Mexican-Americans required that their contribution to North American culture be recognized. At universities located mostly in the West and Southwest, this political activism propelled the creation of programs and departments for Ethnic Studies.

In such circumstances, political activism and artistic production feed each other. On Chicano literature's relation with politics, Cherríe Moraga writes:

> The generation of Chicano literature being read today sprang forth from a grassroots social and political movement of the sixties and seventies that was definitely anti-assimilationist. It responded to a state mandate: art is political. The proliferation of poetry, cuentos, and teatro that grew out of the Movimiento was supported through Chicano cultural centers and publishing projects throughout the Southwest and in every major urban area where a substantial Chicano population resided. The Flor y Canto poetry festival and a teatro that spilled off the flatbed trucks into the lettuce fields in the sixties are the hallmarks of the history of the Chicano cultural movement. Chicano literature was a literature in dialogue with its community. (3)

In comparing the present with the political activism of the sixties and seventies, Moraga observes great differences. Conservative, middle-class concerns have neutralized the political activism, of a period when it was carried out by a working-class Latino student base on university campuses; more and more the literature and its criticism move away from a community-based and political movement (3).

The origin of Chicano theater, as Moraga insinuates, was inseparable from the political and social ideals of the civil rights movements. Aesthetically, Chicano theater, that is, the Teatro Campesino, adopted Brechtian techniques that it incorporated into the cultural and political specificities of the Chicano community. Undoubtedly, of all of the "Hispanic" or "Latino" theaters that have existed in the United States, the Teatro Campesino, which functioned under the directorship of Luis Valdez, is the first to have gained national and international notoriety as a distinctly "Latino" product of a North American context. Moreover, "Hispanic" theater, as Nicolás Kanellos documents in *A History of Hispanic Theatre in the United States:Origins to 1940,* flourished in several cities densely populated by Spanish-speaking people. In this country, from the mid-nineteenth century until the late sixties, Teatro Campesino was the first to represent, on a national scale, a segment of the Latino community; it is also the first group to have inspired the formation of other Latino theater groups across the country. Another important difference between the theatre that flourished in the late 1960s and the new performances documented in Kanellos's study is to be found in the old theater's reliance on travelling acting troupes and on plays from Spanish-speaking countries. While these performances entertained "Latino" or "Hispano" populations in the United States, the artistic and thematic genesis of these productions did not necessarily confront, adopt, or recognize in any significant manner the North American context in which these events were performed. In light of this situation, one appreciates the political and cultural significance of the theater that flourished in the 1960s: this was an oppositional theater, an arm of the Chicano movement to resist cultural and economic domination and an expression of Chicano cultural affirmation.

While the aesthetic innovations and political merits of the Teatro Campesino are commendable, its early dramatic productions are, from a feminist perspective, problematic. Chicana critics Yolanda Broyles-González and Yvonne Yarbro-Bejarano have called attention to the boundaries placed on women's participation in the "teatro." Broyles-González's historical research and personal interviews with the women involved in these dramatic productions reveal that in the course of the "teatro"'s evolutionary process from "actos" to "mitos" to "corridos," from the days of the "actos" performed by farmworkers for farmworkers atop flatbed trucks to the days of *Zoot Suit* in Hollywood and on Broadway, the female characters remained limited to stylized types: 1) women solely defined by their familial category: mothers, sisters, or wife/girlfriend; 2) female characters monotonously divided into one of the two quintessential sexual categories: whores or virgins; 3) one-dimensional stereotypes whose roles do not permit the dramatic space necessary for the unfolding of a full character; 4) and roles invariably limited to secondary; i.e., accessory to those of the male characters. Never would the world be seen through women's eyes (164). While a few women involved with the group tried to resist these limitations, even the most recent widely viewed performance, the "Corridos," which was aired on television through the Public Television Network, continued to place women in stereotypical roles not significantly different from those performed in the early moments of "actos."[2]

In the attempt to add a voice about the struggle against gender oppression to the initial struggles of the "teatro," several collective theaters of women emerged, and Chicana writers began to experiment with the dramatic genre more consistently. Valentina Productions, located in the San Francisco Bay area, and "Las Comadres," on the San Diego border, are collectives of women "teatristas" who address women's issues openly. Further compounding the problems faced by a women's theater is the extra challenge placed on women entering a profession that demands, during touring engagements, a significant amount of time away from the home and children. Few women have the luxury to meet these requisites.

Although each adopts different positions in regards to dramaturgy and issues of feminism, race, class, and self-identity, Estela Portillo Trambley in El Paso, Texas, Cherríe Moraga in the Bay area, and Dolores Prida and Maria Irene Fornes in New York are artists whose pioneering dramatic productions have contributed to the creation of a "Latino" or "Hispanic" presence in North American theater.[3]

Women of Color and Theater

Women of color, a term originated in the 1970s to represent a challenge to the presumed homogeneity of voice and vision within the feminist movement, designates a political position that identifies North American women who face the triple burden of class, racial, and gender oppression. Women of color's contribution to the theater has been to bring to center stage their histories, traditions, and experiences, which affect the way they write for the theater, the way they choose to practice their art. Native-American women, for example, reclaim their storytelling traditions. Because people of color are too often examined, defined, and labeled through the historical legitimation of the European-American perspective that renders all other perspectives secondary or inferior, a common thread that unifies the minority women playwrights who embrace the political term "women of color" is that, in one form or another, they attempt to validate cultural forms, histories, languages, and traditions of people not fully incorporated and recognized in the dominant European-American culture. In using the term "political," I am not referring solely to actions originating in the government; rather, I wish to evoke the everyday negotiations of power, economics, ethics, education, culture, race, class, gender, emotions, intellect, and art that Amerasian playwright Valina Hasu Houston aptly designates as "the politics of life" (8).

African-American women have been the pioneers and the first spokespersons of the movement of women of color. Similarly, they were the first women of color to achieve commercial and critical success in theater circles. Alice Childress' play *Trouble in Mind* won the Obie award in 1956 for the best Off-Broadway play of the season. In 1959,

Lorraine Hansberry's *A Raisin in the Sun* won the New York Drama Critics Circle's award for best play of the year. Adrienne Kennedy, in 1964, earned an Obie Distinguished Play award for *Funnyhouse of a Negro.* And in 1970, Ntozake Shange's *for colored girls who have considered suicide when the rainbow is enuf* was a commercial success on Broadway. While most of these playwrights center their work on their experiences as black women, some explore the position of African-American women and mainstream theater. By mainstream theater, I refer to large commercial houses and theaters that mainly produce plays written by European-American male authors or by deceased European playwrights. Alice Childress' *Florence* (1949) and *Trouble in Mind* dramatize the oppression African-American actors endure within their profession. In *Florence,* the protagonist's only opportunities are to be cast in a Broadway play in which she performs the marginal role of a maid or to work in all-black productions, thus separated from the dominant culture.

Adrienne Kennedy has further explored the complex relationship between African-American women and the dominant white theater establishment. In the 1976 play *A Movie Star Has to Star in Black and White,* the protagonist, Clara, is an African-American dramatist who experiences difficulties in writing plays true to her complex life experience, that is, with black characters. Hollywood's all-white glamorous actors and actresses constantly encroach on Clara's imagination, affecting her ability to write stories with black "stars" since the dominant culture has not allowed her to visualize African-Americans as "Hollywood Stars." In this play, as in *The Owl Answers,* Kennedy insinuates the effects of internal racism on colonized people. She also shows the marginality and invisibility people of color experience in the dominant culture.

Making history's "invisibilities" visible is one way to describe Velina Hasu Houston's early work. In the trilogy of plays that culminated with *Tea,* Houston treats events of American history not always acknowledged in contemporary classrooms. In *Tea,* she examines critically the way traditional Japanese culture perceived the women who married American soldiers during World War II. Yet, the author maintains that same captious glance at the discriminatory relocation policies the U.S. government imposed on the Japanese Americans and the Amerasian communities during World War II. Houston, who is the daughter of a Japanese international bride and an African-American/Native-American father, in her personal life is engaged with community activist groups that promote the understanding of Amerasian culture. While the playwrights of color discussed thus far practice their art and political positions in various fashions, their work manifests how race, class, and gender affect the art and personal experience of individuals of that background.

Subverting Scripts: Performing Border Identities. Unlike other women of color who are monolingual and write monolingual drama, some bilingual Latina playwrights who decide to write in English and Spanish run the risk of linguistically marginalizing themselves even further from mainstream audiences and theater. Most Latina playwrights today choose to write almost entirely in English with a few words in Spanish or Spanglish, the mixture of Spanish and English and the form of speech more in tune with their personal experiences and with the form of speech spoken by the largest segment of the Latino community. But language, culture, and value systems are, at times, so interconnected that their separation is impossible. Take, for example, *Coser y cantar* by Cuban American playwright Dolores Prida, where the dialects of Cuban identity and Anglo-American assimilation are dramatized by having the protagonist split into two: one in English and the other in Spanish, both selves competing to dominate the creation of a whole. Prida, in a gesture that simultaneously embodies a sense of gleefulness and irony, describes her play *Coser y cantar* as one "which deals with how to be a bilingual, bicultural woman in Manhattan and keep your sanity . . ." ("The Show" 185). Nevertheless, even if a play is written in English with a few words in Spanish, the other language, the other culture is still ever present.

Simply María or the American Dream is a play that depicts the conflicting messages that two cultures—Anglo-American and Mexican—offer to a young woman caught between them. What emerges is the creation of an identity neither wholly one nor the other; it partakes of both. This experimental play adopts a nonlinear structure, presenting a series of episodes heralded by titles that unsettle the audience's expectation of suspense. Borrowing from Brecht's notion of epic theater, it is a direct political critique of representational structures that mystify social relations. Dismantling the contrived nature of realist drama and its ideological implications, epic theater aims to empower its audiences by showing them that in realist drama, as in life, hidden power structures manipulate the construction of the real.

Stressing narrativity rather than plot, *Simply María* appropriates North American and Latin American popular culture but not without subverting these forms before incorporating them into the text. Its thematic ethnic content, as occurs in some recent Chicano films, functions as a formal element that creates a style unto itself (see Noriega 154). *Simply María* performs on stage the creation of a Latina American identity; in both form and content, this new bilingual/bicultural creation challenges dominant discourses, as it reflects the social and political oppression people of color endure in the United States.

In contrast with the earliest dramatic performances on North American soil and with the more contemporary Chicano theater of Luis Valdez, where the presence of women is narrowed to their participation as actresses in secondary roles, *Simply María* centers on a young woman's search for independence from the ponderous cultural impositions placed on women by the traditional Mexican culture.[4] Ultimately, the heroine's quest is for the happiness promised by the American dream.

Dissenting from narratives that inundate popular culture, *Simply María* is antiromantic. In this one-act play divided into twelve scenes, the literary encoding of the mise-en-scène is highlighted by constant references to popular culture's romantic scripts, as is evident in the first part of the play's title, *Simply María,* which alludes to *Simplemente María,* an extremely popular "telenovela" that aired across Latin America and in the United States through the Spanish International Network (SIN). As is characteristic of most popular soap operas, *Simplemente María* draws on the Cinderella theme of the beautiful young woman from the lower class who raises her socioeconomic status through marriage to a wealthy man (Antola and Rogers 289-95). In contradistinction to the Latin American version, the unromantic narrative of *Simply María* is compared with the universal narrative of North American culture—the American dream. Thus, it evokes the hybrid nature of this creation. In addition, by equating the felicity that the American dream brings to mind with the title of a soap opera, a melodrama, it foreshadows the specific North American reception of Latin Americans, particularly the poorer and more ethnically marked, a differentiation that, as I will argue later, is based on racial grounds. Yet, the deployment of popular narratives, to which the play's title alludes, is not an isolated instance; rather, it highlights the beginning of a technique used consistently throughout the play.

The nonlinear structure of the text begins with the end; in a flashback, María enters the stage and sits down to watch the enactment of the creation of her adult character. In regards to the theatrical performance, this strategy foregrounds the fact that the audience can no longer maintain the illusion of being the unseen spectator at an event which is really taking place. Scene 1, set in a small village in Mexico, recreates the night María's parents eloped, an act conceived in the imagination of María's mother with expectations advanced by popular romantic tales. The escape of María's parents, Ricardo and Carmen, is introduced with an allusion to the primordial romantic narrative: "Romeo and Juliet elope" (117). But Carmen's running away from her mother's home is a distant reenactment of the fiction on which it is modeled. On the night Carmen descends from her balcony to meet Ricardo, she asks him for the horse they will need for their flight. Instead of a horse, Ricardo has brought his old bike. Carmen reacts incredulously: "Qué! On that? No! How could you . . . Everyone knows that when you elope, you elope on a horse, not on a . . . Ricardo, you promised!" (117). Still, they escape on a ragged bicycle that with difficulty accommodates its two passengers. On one level, this scene elucidates the way in which popular culture informs the imagination and expectations of some people, that is, "the way things should be." López, in counterpoint, deconstructs these narratives by representing an outcome that is more realistic. In this initial framing scene, the playwright posits a theme that recurs throughout the rest of the theatrical performance: scripts are scripts and, as such, they can be rewritten.

Another manifestation of popular culture that *Simply María* blends into the construction of the play is film. Ricardo, in a charro's attire, engaged in the act of rescuing his young daughter and wife from the mob and confusion of downtown Los Angeles, borrows from the Mexican tradition of charro movies, in which the hero is always a man dressed in that sort of outfit. Even amidst the array of characters that stroll through L.A.'s Broadway—preachers, street vendors, Chicano activists, Valley Girls, cholos, and bag ladies—Ricardo's entrance into this scene is monumental and a bit out of synchrony with the urban setting. His arrival is described thus: "Ricardo, dressed in a charro outfit, enters and gives some yells as if ready to sing a corrido. All the chaos of the city stops, and all the city people recoil in fear" (123). In contrast to the scene in which Ricardo's and Carmen's realities override the romantic tale, the fictitious film narrative in this case nullifies the plausibilities of fact. López, in a sense, deploys this strategy to validate

Performing Border Identities

the Mexican cultural presence in this foreign land: only in the fantastic realm of the movies could a poor Mexican man be endowed with the heroic stature described in this scene; only in the movies could an otherwise vulnerable foreigner cause such an uproar in a setting designated by the title projected onto the back wall of the stage, "Los Angelitos del Norte". This scene, akin to the one analyzed previously, points to the double cultural reading encoded in this text.

The "telenovelas" intertext recurs in scene 9. Soon after a confrontation with her parents, who want María to relinquish her ambition to attend college and urge her, instead, to find a nice man to marry, María falls sleep. The three following scenes take place in her dreams. She sees herself married to a man who treats her like a domestic servant and objectifies her as his sexual commodity. In her nightmare, a pregnant María one day sits in her living room to watch a T.V. soap opera, "Happily Ever After." The heroine of this story, Eliza Vásquez, is in the midst of walking out on a suffocating marriage and confronts her husband, Devero, with her dissatisfaction and desire to be free. "But I've given you everything!" says Devero, to which Eliza responds: "Everything but an identity! Well, Devero, Devero, Devero, I've discovered I no longer need you. There are unfulfilled dreams I must pursue. I want adventure" (133). The commercial that interrupts this segment of the soap opera ridicules the ideal traditional domestic wife: it shows a husband returning home from work with a precious gift for his wife—a can of Ajax—a gift the wife receives claiming it is an unmerited proof of her husband's devotion and generosity towards her.

The self-reflexive element of these scenes necessitates further discussion: the soap opera and T.V. commercial sequences have been taped in María's living room and not in a T.V. studio. When in her dream María sees a T.V. producer and actors in her apartment, she timidly protests their intrusion in her house but easily acquiesces and lets the show be performed into her living room. Thus, María watches a "fictive" resolution to the dilemmas affecting decisions that she should make when she awakens. Moreover, we, the audience of the play, are voyeurs of María's soap opera watching. In the theatrical event, this episode calls attention to the constructed nature of representation.

Interestingly, "Happily Ever After" does not honor the implied, anticipated ending alluded to by its title. Instead, it illustrates that this narrative is dispensed at great expense to women. The T.V. commercial that performs a cheerful version of the satisfied domestic wife underscores the disparity with the ending of "Happily Ever After."

López, in this manner, highlights the fact that women's roles and behavior are scripts constructed and imposed by a patriarchal ideology. From a different angle, given that community ethnic theaters are most likely sources for producing this play and that the audience in attendance would most probably be Latino, López's self-referential technique of voyeurism performs for the Latino community the construction of a bilingual/bicultural identity, an alternative model nonexistent in the dominant culture.

"Happily Ever After" further explores the multicultural dimensions of North American society: the bicultural nature of this television production is not yet found in the North American version of soap operas nor in the Latin American "telenovela." From the Latin American "telenovela," it borrows its clear-cut ending format that in its North American counterpart remains open (López 8). Yet, thematically it departs from the romantic Cinderella theme common among Latin American "telenovelas." Furthermore, by performing on stage the type of domestic problems that frequently arise after the amorous "happy ending," it demystifies romantic closures. From North America, it appropriates the cheerful notion of a "happily ever after." However, in staging Latinos as central characters in what appears as mainstream soap opera, it breaks boundaries placed on the representation of Latinos in Anglo-American television: no North American soap opera, to date, has permitted Latinos to be central characters of their stories.[5] "Happily Ever After" draws on both cultural traditions. A tinge of ironic playfulness accompanies the appropriations from North American popular culture: the barrio in which the poor, undocumented Mexican people live, among them María and her parents, is announced by a slide that reads "The Little House in the Ghetto." This, of course, alludes to the "All American" (White/European) family of the North American popular television series "The Little House on the Prairie." The racial differences and their consequences are implicit in the shift.

These self-referential dramatic techniques beg for a closer examination of the construction of scripts, particularly those that have circumscribed women's lives. In scene 2, a slide reading "The Making of a Mexican Girl" advances the revelation of this creation. The wedding of María's parents as well as her infant baptism occur in the same ceremony under the tutelage of the Catholic church. As the priest places the baby in the center of the altar, three angelic girls sing beautifully the word "María," followed by a recitation of the ingredients for "making a Mexican girl." From a long list, I summarize the following examples: 1) as a nice girl María ought to be forgiving and obedient . . . ; 2) she ought to like dolls, kitchens, cleaning, and caring for children . . . ; 3) María ought not to be independent nor to enjoy sex but must endure it in order to bear children . . . ; 4) she never ought to shame her society . . . ; and most importantly, 5) her goal in life is to reproduce; her only purpose in life is to serve three men: father, husband, and son (119).

The resonance in this trio of men of the Holy Trinity of the Catholic church—the Father, the Son, and the Holy Spirit—is not gratuitous. For the church, aside from offering its blessing, prescribes this behavior for women.[6] In the scene depicting María's dream, where she is marrying the "nice man" chosen by her parents, the sermon of the Catholic wedding ceremony dismantles the true essence of the type of traditional matrimony María is expected to accept. The priest intones:

> . . . María, do you accept José Juan González López as your lawfully wedded husband to love, cherish, serve, cook for, clean for, sacrifice for, have his children, keep his house, love him even if he beats you, commits adultery, gets drunk, rapes you lawfully, denies you your identity, money, love his family, serve his family, and in return ask for nothing? (132)

Significantly, the baptism takes place in the Mexican village where María was born. The cultural baggage of these scripts will accompany María's growth into womanhood, creating a source of conflict with American society's freer values in regards to women. Together with her mother, María arrives in the United States as a small child; she comes to join her father, who since Carmen's pregnancy has been saving money to send for his wife and child. Like that of many poor immigrants, Ricardo's reason for asking his wife and child to join him is to be able to offer them a better future. "In America," Ricardo tells his young child, "the education is great. You can take advantage of all the opportunities offered to you. You can work hard to be just as good as anybody" (124). Little María believes her father's words and begins to adapt gradually to U.S. values by showing a spirit of competitiveness in school sports and academics, behavior that her mother distrusts as unbefitting of a Mexican girl. María's adolescence slips away in a constant battle between, on one hand, her parents' demand that she excel in domestic chores and, on the other, her yearnings for independence and the opportunity to go to college.

It is not accidental, then, that María will want to go to college to study to be an actress. For what is acting but the ability to transcend oneself, to become another person by performing a different script? Yet, this emphasis on acting in *Simply María* and in *Latina,* as I will discuss later, goes beyond the use of game-playing as a mere theatrical convention, as some critics have observed to be the case of contemporary Latin American theater (e. g., Bixler). On the use of game-playing by Latin American women playwrights, Catherine Larson observes:

> They have self-consciously incorporated games into their plays' structures to highlight from a woman's perspective the theme that life, as well as intheater, is a game . . . When the entire drama consists of games within games, when characters knowingly assume roles inside of roles and "stage" plays inside the play itself, the dramatist underscores such concepts as the nature of human identity, the relationship between the theater and reality, and the methods by which authority and control are manifested and maintained in real life . . . (77-78)

Rather than espousing the idea that life, like theater, is a game, López views the similarities between life and theater more as an enactment of scripts that are embedded in the culture in which a woman finds herself. When those narratives prove inadequate, she has the potential to rewrite them. *Simply María,* it seems to me, is more in tune with Elizabeth Burns' conception of

> A theatrical quality of life . . . experienced more concretely by those who feel themselves at the margins of events either because they have adopted the role of spectator or . . . because they have not been offered a part or have not learnt it sufficiently well to enable them to join the actor—those who do not participate in a social system are less likely to see it as natural and are therefore more sensitive to its contrived or constructed quality. (11)

The notion of life as a game embodies a sense of playfulness that, while having the potential to highlight relations of power, does not necessarily show how to change them. Moreover, Burns' comment contextualizes María's marginality in both Mexican and American cultures. The role she ought to play is not yet written in either culture; she must write it herself. Once that script is written, she can empower herself by performing it, no longer confined to limbo by the confusion of not having an identity, a role to play.

The empowerment gained by performing a Latina identity can be appreciated when one considers that from the perspective of a woman of color, of a Latina within the North American context, acting out roles

Performing Border Identities 85

signifies one channel through which she can change the negative Latino images produced by Hollywood and Broadway. Sarita, an actress and the central character of Milcha Sánchez-Scott's play *Latina,* echoing Alice Childress' *Florence,* voices the predicament of Latino actors by evoking the sort of Latino images on mainstream television programming. She laments:

> I'll give you my credits. I was a barrio girl who got raped in Police Story, a young barrio mother who got shot by a gang in Starsky and Hutch, a barrio wife who got beat up by her husband who was in a gang in Rookies. I was even a barrio lesbian who got knifed by an all girl gang called the Mal-flores . . . that means Bad Flowers. It's been a regular barrio blitz on television lately. If this fad continues, I can look forward to being a barrio grandmother done-in by a gang of old Hispanics called Los Viejitos Diablitos, the old devils . . . . (89)

While, as Sarita observes, Latino actors still find their substance constrained by the desires of European-American producers, once a Latino actress/actor is well established within mainstream media, she/he has the potential to exercise influence to modify the negative images of Latinos circulated by Hollywood and Broadway.[7] Josefina López's own aspiration to be a writer was born, precisely, of her desire to change the negative images Hollywood and Broadway circulate of Latinos and especially Latinas (*Real Women* 44).

Acting plays a pivotal role in *Simply María* and *Latina.* In Sánchez-Scott's play, the emphasis on performing assumes varied shapes that all lead to one end: empowerment. 1) Sarita's fear that she might not get a part in the T.V. series for which she auditioned because, as she says, "I am too dark and freaky for Eight is Enough. They don't have stupid Mexicans playing nurses on prime time, you know I might scare the kids," is, by the end of the play, dissipated because she is finally cast in a nonstereotypical Latina role (93). 2) To support her acting career, Sarita works as a counselor for a domestic agency located in downtown Los Angeles, where the multiethnic composition of that city is, once more, highlighted. But unlike *Simply María,* which draws primarily on Mexican and Chicano presence and cultural forms, that is, cholos, Chicano activists, and Mexican corridos, through *Latina*'s domestic agency circulate women from all over Latin America: Cubans, Peruvians, Salvadorians, Colombians, and Guatemalans, among others. Some of these women are undocumented and can barely speak English. To help them find employment, Sarita, in several instances, plays the employer and teaches them how to "act" more American in order to fit their European-American employers' demands. 3) In her role as a counselor, Sarita functions as a broker between the recently immigrated poor women and their white employers.

Through the play several European-Americans complain about their maids' inability to perform to their standards. On one occasion, an employer returns Almita, the maid that worked for her, as if she were damaged merchandise, to the domestic agency, claiming that "She has no respect for my blue and white Chinese porcelain, or any of our antiques and things that are irreplaceable . . ." (109). A critique of the objectification of human beings and the human value attached to objects in consumer societies is invoked in this brief exchange. Still, Sarita never defends the maids, taking, instead, the side of the employer and by doing so provokes resentment from the Latina women who interpret Sarita's actions as a sign that she is ashamed of being a Latina and wants to be a "gringa desteñida" (112). Here, it is worth recalling Katheryn Rios' study, discussed in the introduction, for the character of Sarita clearly embodies the sort of advantages—acculturated demeanor, citizenship—that an illegal, poor woman from South America lacks in the U. S. context. In the final scene, Sarita for the first time stands up for the Latina women by rebutting the unjust accusations of an employer, engaging in physical contact with the aggressor. The Latina women applaud Sarita's efforts to defend them; one of them affirms: "Sarita, I only wanted you to stand up for us, not to kill the woman. Andale un abrazo . . . Ahora, sí eres una latina completamente latina" (140). According to this character, in order to become a complete Latina, action is required: "Acting" Latina, according to this definition, means acting in opposition to the forces that cause the oppression to the most disempowered. Not taking action, not standing-up for the rights of the more marginalized and vulnerable is viewed by the immigrant women as "acting" white.

The interesting aspect of these three examples is that the value attached to acting derives from its practical purposes in seeking to empower the disempowered. Everyday "acts" constitute Houston's "politics of life." Yet, in essence, they are not radically different from the performative act theory advanced by Judith Butler. Although stressing sexuality and gender construction, Butler postulates that gender

> . . . Is an identity tenuously constituted in time—an identity instituted through a stylized repetition of acts. Further, gender is instituted

> through the stylization of the body and, hence, must be understood as the mundane way in which bodily gestures, movements, and enactments constitute the illusion of an abiding gendered self. (270-71)

Simply María and *Latina* provide examples of a similar type of "performative acts" proposed by Butler's theory. Besides, López's and Sánchez-Scott's "acts" seek to change the artistic and social world they inhabit. For actors and playwrights, Hollywood and Broadway are sites in need of much change.

Simply María intimates reasonable root causes for Hollywood's acceptance of Latinos. Scene 3 stages the qualitatively different reception the Statue of Liberty dispenses to the European immigrant and to the non-European, in this case, the Mexicans. A giant sail enters the stage brought on by four European immigrants: an Italian, French, German, and Anglo; they all wave goodbye to their countries in their native languages. In the background the sound of "America the Beautiful" plays while three Mexican immigrants enter the stage. Ricardo is one of them. The Statue of Liberty recites the well-known verse:

> Give me your tired, your poor, your huddled masses yearning to breathe free . . . I give you life, liberty and the pursuit of happiness for the price of your heritage, your roots, your history, your relatives, your language . . . Conform, adapt, bury your past, give up what is yours and I'll give you the opportunity to have what is mine. (120-21)

Two of the Mexican immigrants accept this promise; one of them responds: "Pues bueno, if we have to" (121). As lights flash representing the celebration of the Americanization of the European immigrants, those same flickers become the glints of the helicopters that hunt the Mexican immigrants; the helicopters' lights are accompanied by the barking of hounds. The European immigrants join the Statue of Liberty in pointing to the Mexicans so that they get caught. The scene ends with the European immigrants standing proudly next to the U.S. icon, while the Mexicans run offstage. As performed in this scene, there are no differences between the European and the Mexican immigrants except for race or color. Both groups are willing to abide by the demands of the North American foundational promise; yet, the Mexicans are not welcomed.

But López is not the first playwright to point to the difference between North America's reception to the European and the non-

European; other North American artists of color have made the same type of critique of the ideals of the Statue of Liberty. Amerasian writer Susy So Schaller in her poem "Forget Me Not America" describes the sense of broken promises experienced by many Amerasians. Extrapolating from these examples and from the constraints of North American history, one may extend this sentiment to immigrants of color, most particularly to those who are poor. Addressing the Statue of Liberty, "Forget Me Not America" reads:

> ... as you flock by the thousands to pay tribute
> to a statue who represents your beloved ideals
> falling short of our ideals,
> have we settled for idle worship
> making pilgrimage to stone?
> ... America, you fight for the first breath of
> the unborn loose chains of your forgotten children
> who remain wealthy heirs to two countries
> yet without a home to call their own
> whose only claim is an unmapped destiny
> in a forgotten country called Amerasia.

Schaller's poem, in the second stanza, eloquently invokes the invisibility, the "unmapped destiny" of Amerasians left behind in Asia. The first stanza voices the sense of betrayal that Amerasians, like other people of color, often experience in this country. Likewise, López hints that the Statue of Liberty and the other immigrants do not welcome the Mexicans because they are not white Europeans. A similar attitude explains why the head nurse who delivers María's babies, the ones she gives birth to during the nightmare sequence, refers to them as "Mexican litter" (136). To borrow the title from Cornell West's book, in North American society, as in Brazil and as in most societies, "race matters."

Josefina López's critique of North American prejudiced practices is mild in comparison to other women writers of color such as Audre Lorde, Patricia Williams, bell hooks, Gloria Anzaldúa, and Cherríe Moraga. López in this play never makes direct reference to race; rather, she quietly exposes representations of how that prejudice is enacted. Yet, neither María nor López can disassociate themselves from the implications brought about by their "raced" body in dominant white America. María's last words on stage as she prepares to abandon her parents' household in search of her independence are telling: "Mexico is in my blood and America is in my heart" (141). While both Mexico and the U.S. are equated with bodily organs, the heart is commonly associated with a state of mind, a set of ideas and values. Blood, in contrast, evokes, among many other things, a graphic color often associated with violence; it cannot be easily ignored: it is always a strong, notorious differential marker.

The cultural confusion between the Mexican and North American value systems that the play chronicles allows María to turn that confusion into a source of agency that gives her the courage to abandon her parents' household. North America has rewarded María's academic hard work by granting her a four-year scholarship to attend college. When María awakes from her sleep, she overhears her mother's cries as she argues with her husband. Carmen is confronting Ricardo about her suspicion of his infidelity; although initially he attempts to deny these accusations, Ricardo admits to his wife: "Look, every man sooner or later does it" (140). Their argument reveals that Ricardo has been unfaithful to his wife many times before; Carmen knew this but chose to remain passive out of fear that her husband would send her and María back to Mexico (140).[8] María recognizes that within the Mexican cultural framework this is the type of future that awaits her if she is to follow her parents' cultural values. Had she remained in the Mexican village in which she was born, María most likely would have had no options but to follow the traditional Mexican script. Yet, she is in North America; she opts to fight for her share of the American dream, accepting the college scholarship that will separate her from her parents:

> I want to create a world of my own. One that combines the best of me. I won't forget the values of my roots, but I want to get the best of this land of opportunities . . . Los quiero mucho. Nunca los olvidaré. Mexico is in my blood . . . And America is in my heart. (141)

Mexican and North American societies, values, and popular narratives are, indeed, the procreators of *Simply María*. While on one level *Simply María* is celebratory of North American values, a counternarrative represents critically the racial prejudices dispensed to the non-European population.

The mainstream audience's reception of ethnic theater is indicative that North American society is still slow to accept cultural artifacts from traditions other than the white European. As mentioned before, López's plays have been produced in California by community theaters, that is, in ethnically based productions. Among the community of Chicano theater scholars, the work of Josefina López has begun to be better known, thanks especially to the theater organization Teatros Nacionales de Aztlán (TENAZ), but Anglo-American companies have yet to take interest in producing this play.[9] Perhaps their reluctance to undertake ethnic projects derives from the fear that they will not prove to be commercially successful ventures: the plays are too "ethnic" for white audiences. To a certain extent, it is true that ethnic plays tend to treat themes, cultural and linguistic forms that, in order to be fully appreciated, require explanation of their context.

African-American playwrights like Lorraine Hansberry, Adrienne Kennedy, and Ntozake Shange have had successful mainstream dramatic productions. In regards to Hispanic American women playwrights, Maria Irene Fornes, born in Cuba of European extraction, is the most respected and admired among the Off-Broadway, experimental theater circles, but Fornes' plays often do not deal with Latin American or Hispanic American themes; rather, her most successful works, among them the play that won her an Obie award, *Fefu and Her Friends,* are about middle-class European Americans. Cherríe Moraga's theater of commitment stands in striking contrast to Fornes' work.[10]

These observations should not diminish Josefina López's artistic and personal achievements. With all the limitations encountered in North America by a poor immigrant of color, where else could López, who lived undocumented in this country until a few years ago, at her youthful age, achieve so much? The character of María is, after all, López's own alter ego: *Simply María* draws heavily on autobiography. A native of Cerritos, San Luis Potosí, in Mexico, López came to this country with her parents when she was six years old. Now in her late twenties, she has captured numerous awards, and is currently the most produced Latina playwright; López's work has been received warmly by some local newspapers (Churnin). López identifies personally with the political label of a Chicana and views her role as a Chicana playwright as a commitment to changing the negative representations of Latinos, and especially Latinas, in the theater and in Hollywood (*Real Women* 44). Like María's decision to seek the fulfillment of the American dream, López's accomplishments as a writer are the fruits of the author's search for that dream. Like the heroine of *Simply María,* artistically and personally López has created her own world, one that combines the best of the scenarios she inhabits. For a change, the heroine of a play is an intelligent, independent Latina who demystifies Anglo-American images of Latina women.[11] In *Simply María* the Latino community has a playwright and a heroine to celebrate, and North America procreates a raced, gendered version of the Horatio Alger narrative.

Simply María and *Latina* draw from the author's personal experiences, dramatizing the creation of a Latina identity. In this regard, they echo Cuban American dramatist Dolores Prida, who affirms: "most of my plays have been about the experience of being a Hispanic in the United States, about people trying to reconcile two cultures and two languages and two visions of the world into a particular whole: plays that aim to be a reflection of a particular time and space, of a here and now" ("The Show" 182). Like López, Milcha Sánchez-Scott immigrated to the United States, to Los Angeles specifically, as a small child. Sánchez-Scott's ancestry is Colombian, Indonesian, Dutch, and Chinese, but, because her upbringing in California was heavily influenced by Chicano culture, she adopted that label for herself. *Latina,* like *Simply María,* draws from the author's personal experiences. In her more recent play, *Roosters,* Sánchez-Scott recovers her South American roots; she experiments with magic realism in a piece where the fictional space is an unspecified place in the Southwest. However, the incorporation of other Latin American elements can be traced to her first play, *Latina:* the characters are immigrants from various Latin American nations and not simply from Mexico. Peruvian music accompanies the beginning and the end of the play; references to the sculptures of Mexican/Costa Rican artist Francisco Zúñiga are a source of proud cultural identification to a young Sarita, who is struggling to find her identity. These examples illustrate that Latino ethnicities are complex and continuously evolving but that the term Latino as opposed to Hispanic allows commonalties to surface: working-class identification is an important one.

In both *Simply María* and *Latina* class needs to be addressed with regards to the theme of the play and the playwright's background. The working-class context of López's play explains in part, the structural use of narratives produced for mass consumption, such as soap operas, movies, and T.V. series. Aside from the literary allusion to *Romeo and Juliet,* a narrative so common that its reference is hardly restricted to a literary source, there are no other literary evocations. Furthermore, the predominance of popular culture in *Simply María* invokes a postmodern gesture that breaks boundaries between high and low art by indiscriminately incorporating popular cultural forms into what, in the modernist sense, would be high art.

Latina dramatizes the exploitation of maids from their perspective, as opposed to their employer's, as was the case in the

Brazilian play, *Lua nua*. Clara, one of the characters of *Latina*, describes her employer:

> She like to talk. Eso de everybody equal. She go to meet with the other women, they talk talk everybody equal y de los husbands y como los hombres le tratan de mal. They talk how the women must be equal to men. Then she come to me and say, "Clara, you and me, equal." Hmmmmmph! I don't pay attention . . . She don't know nothing. I been taking three buses every day to clean houses for fifteen years and she . . . (116)

Another character, Chata, articulates her own version of women of color's complaint to the white feminist movement: "Comadre, you ain't equal to her. Any pendejo can see that" (116). The dehumanization of the domestic worker that Dulce in *Lua nua* was not able to voice is expressed in *Latina* by Lola's confrontation with her employer:

> Why, no one in your house call me by my name. . . all of you speak of me as your Mexican maid. Always you say, "Ask the maid, tell the maid." Each day you make me more nobody, more dead. You put me in nice white uniforms so I won't offend your good taste. You take my name, my country. You don't want a person, you want a machine. My name is Lola. I am from Guatemala. (139)

While the Brazilian play presents the white employer, Sílvia, in a sympathetic manner, in *Latina* the European-American employers are harshly represented. Sánchez-Scott clearly criticizes women who seek liberation at the expense of the exploitation of other women. The two North American plays examined in this chapter overtly address issues involving class differences among women in a way that, in comparison to the Brazilian example, the latter only begins to suggest and that the Mexican and Argentine do not treat.

Throughout this discussion, I have been suggesting that narratives—popular, religious, and cultural—inform masked ideologies. At certain moments, those narratives can be appropriated and subverted to show their fictive construction. López's play dismantles popular narratives from the North American and the Latin American cultural spectrums. As a feminist, López pays closer attention to the way those scripts limit women's lives. In *Simply María* she rewrites popular scripts from the Mexican and North American cultures to create a new narrative that will fit neither culture and will subvert both. Rather than writing a story, she opts for the dramatic genre to display how gender roles and cultural values are scripts that can be subverted and rewritten. For, unlike the reading of a story in the privacy of one's home, theater has the advantage of showing, of "putting on stage," the gestation of this new creation. In privileging Brecht's notions of epic theater, López demonstrates how an individual is alterable and able to alter the course of events. She illustrates how performative acts lead to the construction of gendered and cultural identities that are always embedded onto social, cultural, and political contexts and onto structures of power. By performing this bicultural identity, María becomes it.

      Latinas' presence on stage, as evidenced by the works discussed, promises to bring exciting challenges and important contributions to North American theater. These writers incarnate in their dramatic production a mixed blessing: while sitting on the margins of mainstream society, they are, nonetheless, at the forefront of ethnicity and gender awareness. This feature distinguishes them from their counterparts in Latin American countries. As audiences and critics responding to Latinas' dramatic texts, we are moved to ask ourselves questions about the relationship between theater and life, art and society, academic criticism and the social world, because all these realms constitute "the politics of life." In recognizing this challenge, the central remaining question is simply: to act or not to act.

Conclusion

Concluding remarks connote a sense of termination, of closure, that runs counter to the explorations undertaken in this book, since the field that interfaces women playwrights, theater, and feminisms has only recently become the object of critical and, to a lesser extent, pedagogical attention. The special contribution of this study is to fill the scholarly gap existing in the juncture between women's dramaturgy and feminism as they manifest themselves on contemporary stages across the American continent. With the rubric "Americas" I wish to highlight the many linguistic, cultural, and political layers comprising each country that falls under such a heading. This study is limited to the comparative analysis of four countries; however, such a choice does not imply that I believe in the existence of national dramaturges. Rather, the decisions for my choices was guided by pratical considerations, such as finding an adequate methodology. I analyze dramatic texts as theatrical and cultural works, that is, for their thematic and structural aspects as well as establishing ways in which to relate each text to its specific sociocultural context. While this critical framework acknowledges as its locus of enunciation the North American critical context, it crosses geographical, political, social, cultural, and linguistic borders.

For example, the Mexican case study, *Cocinar hombres*, is founded on radical feminism, which underscores women's culture as essentially different and separate from the culture of men. The feminist ideology the play incarnates is manifested through the issue it stages: women's desire, women's sexuality, the flight to a world inhabited only by women, and the construction of a new language, a "feminine" language beyond the confines of patriarchy. The use of stage space and dramatic time departs notoriously from conventional dramatic forms and opens up the possibility of reading the play as representative of a "feminine dramaturgy."

The essentialism on which feminine dramaturgy is predicated must be addressed by acknowledging that *Cocinar hombres* is founded on the ontological presupposition of "Woman" as a universal sign. Difference is framed in the sameness defined by women's separation from men, so that a new monolith is erected from which it is difficult to deviate. Variations of class, race, and culture among women are not accounted for.

The process of subverting heterosexual desire and opening up the possibility for homosexual lust is also predicated on a notion of universality among all women. Like Boullosa's *Cocinar hombres*, the feminist vision of Susana Torres Molina's . . . *Y a otra cosa mariposa* is incarnated in a radical version of feminism in which women's primary relationship is with other women. Unlike the Mexican play, the Argentine example remains within the parameters of conventional dramatic representation. The essence of theater, the mechanisms of substitution enacted through a transvestite index, create a dislocation that destabilizes gender categories, forges a deconstruction of heterosexuality, and normalizes homosexuality within the prevailing social codes. While Boullosa creates a society, a language, and a dramaturgy, Torres Molina's main concern is to challenge the dominant version of sexuality—heterosexuality. As in *Cocinar hombres*, the commonality among women is founded exclusively on their sexual desire. Once more, important aspects that differentiate women, such as social class, race, ethnicity, cultural and linguistic variations, are erased in the construction of all-encompassing theoretical assumptions.

A challenge to the postulations of universal sisterhood among women is staged in the Brazilian play *Lua nua*. The playwright introduces the domestic enterprise to illustrate how its arrangements are symbolic of power relations that cross gender, class, and racial lines. In the play examined, *Lua nua*, the symbolic enactment of power is manifested in the conflicted relationship of dependency between the white, professional, middle-class employer and her working-class colored maid. The playwright introduces the issue of domestic service to challenge any simple notion of woman as a homogenous category united by common oppression and sisterhood. Materialist feminism maintains that women's experience cannot be understood outside of their specific historical, political, and national structure. *Lua nua* stages the functions of class in social arrangements, which means that there are crucial differences between middle-class women and working-class women. From the perspective of the employer, one can apprehend the play as espousing a feminist position, but the presence of the domestic servant calls attention to the limitations of that sort of feminist position. The interface between class and race in Brazilian society is highlighted in this play, as it is also in many instances of the plays written by U.S Latina dramatists.

While in *Lua nua* racially marked women are disempowered, U.S. Latinas, like other women of color in the North American context, struggle to attain agency, equality, justice, and interpretative power. Josefina López's work represents the fruits of this labor. While sitting on the margins of mainstream society, women of color, who are often absorbed into feminist studies that fuse material and radical feminisms, are at the forefront of ethnicity and gender awareness, a feature that distinguishes U.S. Latinas from their counterparts in Latin American countries.

By tracing the diverse manifestations of feminism in theater across the Americas, I have staged critically their common desire to deconstruct patriarchal notions of gendered roles and behavior, of compulsory heterosexuality, and of dramatic forms. These works challenge accepted, androcentric visions of society and art. The plays examined are engaged in a struggle to create a variety of identities, more true to the reality of women's lives. By gaining access to interpretative power they are struggling to create a feminine, if not feminist, dramatic vision. The different forms in which feminist visions are dramatized on stage correspond to the diversity of women that inhabit the American continent.

Unlike the private world of poetry and fiction, drama is the field that has been more male dominated. Its public nature demands a direct confrontation with an audience that has not been, and in many cases is still not, receptive to the presence of women. Through their writing from a woman's perspective, these playwrights remind us that a more complete vision of humanity ought to abandon the limitations of masculine bias and of monolithic ways of being, knowing, and creating. In this book, I have strived to locate writings of women from Sor Juana to María Angélica Ribeiro and contemporary U.S. Latina playwrights in the space they deserve in the annals of criticism as well as in the playhouses: center stage.

ENDNOTES

Introduction

1. I use the term "North America" to refer to institutions and citizens of the United States. While I recognize the falseness of applying this term exclusively to the citizens of this country, I do not know an English equivalent for the Spanish "estadunidense." The term "North America" is equally problematic: Mexico is part of North America and not the same as or similar to the United States and Canada. Besides, "Spanish Americans" prefer "North American" over "American" to designate the citizens of the U.S.

2. I began investigations for this critical enterprise with a research stay in Brazil in September 1991. In October 1994, the field of women playwrights occupied center stage at an international conference, "A Stage of Their Own," focused on Spanish, Latin American, and U.S. Latina dramatists and organized by the University of Cincinnati.

3. I am referring to the first project to set the framework for feminist dramatic history and methodologies. Prior to this study, articles that dealt with women playwrights and feminist analyses of women characters were scattered in theatre reviews, literary journals, and anthologies.

4. See Rosette Lamont's book review.

5. Remarks at a meeting of The Female Dramatic Tradition, Cornell University, spring 1993.

6. Carolyn Law and C. L. Barney Dews call for papers by or about "Working-Class Academics" (PMLA 107 [1992]: 376).

7. Remarks at U. S. Latinos Cultural Studies Colloquium, Cornell University, spring 1991.

8. A good example is Gay Wilentz's work with African and African American women writers. Also El Colegio de la Frontera Norte in Baja California, Mexico and El Colegio de México, among other Mexican institutions, in recent years have begun to have conferences that foster creative and intellectual exchange between Mexican and Chicana writers and critics. Two volumes have been published from the proceedings of such events. See, for example, *Mujer y literatura mexicana y chicana.*

9. The Portuguese colonization of Brazil does not follow the otherwise similar pattern of Spanish American colonies. For more information on Brazil, see C. R. Boxer and Charles Gibson.

10. Fredric Jameson's provocative observation is worth keeping in mind: "We will have to begin to think of the Real, not as something outside of the work, of which the latter stands as an image of representation, but as something born in and vehiculated by the text itself" (81).

11. My sympathy for this study derives partly from my own training as a Hispanist and a Latin Americanist, as is the case with most of the contributors to this collection. Moreover, I gratefully acknowledge Emilie Bergmann's, Gwen Kirkpatrick's, and Francine Masiello's support and encouragement while I was an undergraduate student in their classes. I thank them for practicing in their classroom a feminist pedagogy which quietly demonstrated to me that white women and American women of color are not necessarily, not naturally, antagonistic to each other.

12. For further discussion on changes developing this century, see Franco, "Going Public," and Deutsch.

13. I borrow this phrase from bell hooks' title *Feminist Theory From Margins to Center.*

Chapter One

1. The information in these pages was compiled on a research stay in Brazil from September to December 1991. At that time, no

Endnotes 101

article or book had published the data that I gathered. By my second visit to São Paulo in May 1994, Elza Cunha de Vincenzo's study on contemporary Brazilian women playwrights had been published (1992) in Portuguese by the press of the Universidade de São Paulo, where she did her graudate work under the direction of Renata Pallottini.

2. In a May 1994 interview, Leilah Assunção maintains that Brazilian men continue to perceive the work performed by women, even if they are writers, as secondary. Women's writing is still viewed with the same disrespect that Maria Angélica Ribeiro in the nineteenth century condemned. Ribeiro's exact words are recorded in the introduction to this study.

3. In an excellent documentary that examines Apartheid through the complex relationship between black domestic workers and white South African employers, an employer candidly affirms that they never refer to their servants as "maid" but as "the girl" and "the boy," even employees are older than their employers: they are not adults. This employer concludes that the domestic enterprise consigns blacks to perpetual immaturity and perpetual inferiority. Although Brazil is not South Africa, the ramifications of the domestic enterprise strike me as similar. See Mira Hamermesh's *Madams and Maids.*

4. In the interview cited above, Assunção commented that upon learning the title of a paper I had read at a conference, "In Search of 'empregada doméstica': Public and Private Spheres in Leilah Assunção's *Lua nua,*" she was glad that I had noticed the class issue of "the empregada doméstica." She further mentioned that in Brazil critics had not acknowledged that dimension of her work.

5. The Summer 1993 *Luso-Brazilian Review,* a special issue dealing with Brazilian women and their representation, one finds recent scholarship ranging across various sources such as literature, mass media, and popular culture that supports my arguments.

Chapter Two

1. This observation is based on various sources relating to Argentine theater histories. See Laforgue.

2. For a more detailed survey of women's participation in Argentinean theater circles, see the work of Jean Graham-Jones.

3. I thank Irene Daniel for reminding me of this point.

4. One should note that in his study on gay and lesbian themes in Latin American culture Foster does not include a dramatic text.

Chapter Three

1. Individual chapters devoted to Rosario Castellanos' *El eterno feminino* have been a part of two recent dissertations on contemporary Mexican women writers and Latin American women playwrights. See Roselyn Costantino and Susan Rita Wehling.

2. For further information and analysis on Carmen Boullosa's and Sabina Berman's dramatic production, please see Kirsten F. Nigro and Rosalyn Constantino.

3. The novel *Los amores de Laurita* by Argentine writer Ana María Shua treats this topic explicitly. However, as I discussed in the introduction of this study, the differences between the genres of narrative and theater highlight Boullosa's originality and transgressive gesture.

4. One should note that this is also a common practice in modern male dramatists, for example in the work of Brecht, and Pirandello, to name a few.

5. For feminist criticism deploying this metaphor, see the work of Debra Castillo. With regards to Latin American women writers and the cooking metaphor, a basic but important aspect is often left unexamined: most Latin American women writers have maids to do the cooking for them; they themselves are not

actively engaged in this task. Leilah Assunção's "Interview" confirms this reality in Latin America. Under these circumstances, lower-class women are the ones who do most of the cooking, and yet they are invariably absent from literary production.

6. For a feminist analysis of *Propusieron a María,* see Kirsten F. Nigro and for a postmodern and feminist examination of *Alba y las once mil vírgenes,* see Rosalyn Constantino's "Postomodernism and Feminism."

Chapter Four

1. For further reading on the origins of multicultural America, see the work of historian Ronald Takaki.

2. For an insider's view by a theater practitioner of the early Teatro Campesino, see Yareli Arizmendi's testimony.

3. The labels "Latino" and "Hispanic" are highly debated among those who, because they have roots in different Spanish-speaking countries, are grouped under these labels. "Hispanic," which often includes European Spanish people, is a more congenial term to mainstream society, perhaps, because of its apolitical slant. For new directions in U.S. Latino research, see de la Garza's findings.

4. I am referring particularly to the culture of the small, poor rural villages of Mexico, which tend to be much more traditional than the lower and middle-class segments of Mexican urban centers.

5. There are no references to suggest that it could be a "telenovela" aired through the Spanish International Network and, therefore, be a Latin American "telenovela." Furthermore, given Gutiérrez and Schement's observation, it seems unlikely that the thematic content would lure SIN to program a U.S. Latino soap opera: "Both SIN and the U.S. television networks apparently discriminate against hiring Latinos. Mexican T.V. programs convey value systems that are not always relevant to the U.S. society in which U.S. Latinos live. For instance, surveys of the

U.S. Latino show considerable dissatisfaction with SIN television programs, especially by younger Latinos."

6. Other Chicana writers have denounced the oppressive nature of Catholic teachings as they pertain to women. For further discussion of this topic, see Bettina R. Flores, particularly chapter 7: "Religion, Reality, or Repression."

7. A noteworthy example of an actor who has taken the role of activist is James Edward Olmos, whose participation in movies like The Ballad of Gregorio Cortez and Stand and Deliver, among others, is salient for its nonstereotypical treatment of Latinos. In addition to his efforts to change the images Hollywood produces of Latinos, Olmos is involved with the Latino community's fight against gangs and violence and the challenge of motivating Latino students to obtain an education. Still, many Latino entertainers do not get involved with the community or with political causes because they fear the consequences their actions might have on their future careers and on their survival within the white Hollywood establishment (Nuiry 14-22).

8. It is interesting to note that while *Simply María* challenges dominant negative stereotypes of Latinas, the play supports the stereotype of Latinos as unfaithful men.

9. This comment is made with full awareness that Josefina López's youth is a factor that affects this observation. López wrote her first play, *Simply María,* when she was seventeen; now in her late twenties, she has six plays to her credit. The fifth play, *Unconquered Spirits,* won an honorable mention at the 1992 TENAZ competition. López's latest play, *Confessions of Women From East L.A.,* was staged by El Teatro Campesino in San Juan Bautista, CA, during the summer of 1997.

10. Significantly two Latino shows, the one-man acts of John Leguizamo's *Mambo Mouth* and *Spic-a-rama,* were successful ventures among the Off-Broadway productions; however, these presentations are founded on similar stereotypes perpetuated by mainstream arts and media. The question that comes to mind is

Endnotes 105

whether their mainstream success derives from their perpetuation of these representations and from their failure to challenge them by offering alternative models.

11. Unfortunately, because of its lack of specific Latino cultural references, the character played by Jennifer López, in the movie Out of Sight, cannot be appreciated as a Latina character. López is playing a character of mediterranean descent.

BIBLIOGRAPHY

Ahmad, Aijaz. *In Theory: Classes, Nations, Literatures.* London: Verso, 1992.

Almeida, Décio de. *O teatro brasileiro moderno.* São Paulo: Editora Perspectiva, 1988.

Andrade, Elba and Hilda F. Chamise, eds. *Dramaturgas Latinoamericanas Contemporáneas.* Madrid: Verbum, 1991.

Antola, Livia, and Evere Rogers. "Television Flows in Latin America." *Communication Research* 11 (1984): 183-203.

Appiah, Anthony K. "Is the Post- in Postmodernism the Post- in Postcolonial?" *Critical Inquiry* 17 (1991): 336-57.

Apple, Michael, W. "Series Editor's Introduction." *Racial Formation in the United States: From the 1960s to the 1980s.* Ed. Michael Omi and Howard Winant. New York: Routledge, 1986. vii-xiv.

Arizmendi, Yareli. "La mujer y el teatro chicano." *Mujer y literatura mexicana y chicana.* Ed. Aralia López-González, Amelia Malagamba, and Elena Urrutia. Tijuana, B. C.: El Colegio de la Frontera Norte, 1988. 85-91.

Assunção, Leilah. *Amélia ou roda cor de rosa. Da fala ao grito.* Ed. Moysés Baumstein. São Paulo: Edições Símbolo, 1977. 185-282.

———. *Fala baixo, senão eu grito. Da fala ao grito.* Ed. Moysés Baumstein. São Paulo: Edições Símbolo, 1977. 21-114. 21-114.

———. *Jorginho, o machão. Da fala ao grito.* Ed. Moysés Baumstein. São Paulo: Edições Símbolo, 1977. 115-84.

———. *Lua nua.* São Paulo: Edicões Símbolo, 1977.

———. Personal Interview. May 1994. São Paulo, Brazil.

Austin, Gayle. *Feminist Theories for Dramatic Criticism.* Ann Arbor: U of Michigan P, 1990.

Barreto Leite, Luiza. *A mulher no teatro brasileiro.* Rio de Janeiro: Ediciões Espectáculo, 1965.

Barros, Alcides João de. "A situação da mulher no teatro de Consuelo de Castro e Leilah Assunção." *Latin American Theatre Review 9* (1976): 13-20.

Bauman, Kevin M. "Metatexts, Women, and Sexuality: The Facts and Ph(allacies) in Torres Molina's *Extraño juguete.*" *Romance Languages Annual* 2 (1990): 330-35.

Beauvoir, Simone de. *The Second Sex.* 1952. Trans. and ed. H. M. Parshley. New York: Vintage Books, 1972.

Bell, Steven M. Prolegomenon. *Critical Theory, Cultural Politics, and Latin American Narrative.* Ed. Steven M. Bell, Albert H. Lemay, and Leonard Orr. Notre Dame: U of Notre Dame P, 1993. 1-32.

Bergmann, Emilie. "Sor Juana Inés de la Cruz: Dreaming in a Double Voice." *Women, Culture, and Politics in Latin America: Seminar on Feminism and Culture in Latin America.* Berkeley: U of California P, 1990. 151-72.

———. ed. *Women, Culture and Politics in Latin America: Seminar on Feminism and Culture in Latin America.* Berkeley: U of California P, 1990.

Berlin, Martha. Prologue. *Dueña y señora.* By Susana Torres Molina.Buenos Aires: Ediciones de la Campana, 1993. 5-9.

Berman, Sabina. "El suplicio del placer." *Teatro de Sabina Berman.* México: Editores Mexicanos Unidos, 1985. 266-99.

Bhabha, Homi K. "The Other Question: Difference, Discrimination and the Discourse of Colonialism." *Out There: Marginalization and Contemporary Cultures.* Ed. Russell Ferguson. Cambridge: MIT P, 1990. 76-94.

Bixler, Jacqueline Eyring. "Games and Reality on the Latin American Stage." *Latin American Literary Review* 12 (1988): 22-35.

Bosi, Alfredo. *História concisa da literatura brasileira.* São Paulo: Cultrix, 1991.

Boullosa, Carmen. *Aura y las once mil vírgenes. Teatro herético.* 9-41.

———. *Cocinar hombres. Teatro herético.* 43-82.

———. *Duerme.* Madrid: Alfaguara, 1994.

———. *Llanto: Novelas Imposibles.* México: Ediciones Era, 1992.

———. *Mi versión de los hechos.* México: Arte y Cultura Ediciones, 1987.

———. *Papeles Irresponsables.* México: Juan Pablos Editor, 1989.

———. *Propusieron a María. Teatro herético.* 83-101.

———. *Somos vacas, somos puercos.* México: Ediciones Era, 1991.

———. *Teatro herético.* Puebla, Mexico: Universidad Autónoma de Puebla, 1987.

Boxer, C. R. *The Golden Age of Brazil 1696-1750.* Berkeley: U of California P, 1962.

Bradu, Fabienne. *Señas particulares: escritora.* Mexico: Fondo de Cultura Económica, 1987.

Brecht, Bertolt. "The Modern Theatre is the Epic Theatre." *Dramatic Theory and Criticism: Greeks to Grotowski.* Ed. Bernard Dukore. Orlando, FL: Holt, Rinehart and Winston, 1974. 847-48.

Brookshaw, David. *Race and Color in Brazilian Literature.* Methuen, NJ: Scarecrow, 1986.

Broyles-González, Yolanda. "Women in El Teatro Campesino: 'Apoco Estaba Molacha La Virgen de Guadalupe?'" *Chicana Voices: Intersections of Class, Race and Gender.* Ed. Teresa Córdova. Colorado Springs: National Association of Chicano Studies, 1990. 162-87.

Brownmiller, Susan. *Femininity.* New York: Fawcett Colombine, 1984.

Burns, Elizabeth. *Theatricality.* New York: Harper & Row, 1972.

Butler, Judith. "Gender Trouble, Feminist Theory and Psychoanalytic Discourse." *Feminism/Postmodernism.* Ed. Linda J. Nicholson. New York:Routledge, 1990. 324-40.

―――. "Performative Acts and Gender Constitution: An Essay in Phenomenology and Feminist Theory." *Performing Feminisms: Feminist Theory and Theatre.* Ed. Sue-Ellen Case. Baltimore: Johns Hopkins UP, 1990. 270-82.

Caijao-Salas, Teresa and Margarita Vargas, eds. *Women Writing Women: An Anthology of Spanish American Theater of the 1989's.* Albany: State University of New York, 1997.

Case, Sue-Ellen. *Feminism and Theatre.* New York: Methuen, 1988.

―――. ed. *Performing Feminisms: Feminist Critical Theory and Theatre.* Baltimore: Johns Hopkins UP, 1990.

―――. and Janelle Reinelt, eds. *The Performance of Power: Theatrical Discourse and Politics.* Iowa City: U of Iowa P, 1991.

Castellanos, Rosario. *El eterno femenino.* Mexico: Fondo de Cultura Económica, 1975.

———. *Mujer que sabe latín.* Mexico: Fondo de Cultura Económica, 1984.

Castillo, Debra A. *Talking Back: Toward a Latin American Feminist Literary Criticism.* Ithaca: Cornell UP, 1992.

Castro, Consuelo de. *A flor de pele.* Unpublished script.

———. *O porco ensangrentado.* Unpublished script.

Childress, Alice. *Florence. Masses and Mainstream* 3.10 (1950): 34-57.

———. *Trouble in Mind. Black Theater: A 20th Century Collection. The Work Of Its Best Playwrights.* Comp. Lindsay Patterson. New York: Dodd and Mead, 1971. 135-74.

Churnin, Nancy. "Simply Josefina López." *Los Angeles Times.* July 17, 1990: 8E.

Costantino, Roselyn. "Postmodernism and Feminism in Mexican Theater." *Latin American Theatre Review* 28.2 (1995): 55-71.

———. *Resistant Creativity: Interpretative Strategies and Gender Representation in Contemporary Women's Writing in Mexico.* Diss. Arizona State U, 1992.

Cunha de Vincenzo, Elza. *Um teatro da mulher: Dramaturgia feminina no palco brasileiro contemporâneo.* São Paulo: Edusp, 1992.

Cypess, Sandra Messinger. "La dramaturgia femenina y su contexto socio-cultural." *Latin American Theatre Review* 13.2 (1980): 63-67.

De la Garza, Rodolfo O. "Researchers Must Heed New Realities When They Study Latinos in the U.S." *The Chronicle of Higher Education* June 2, 1993: B2-B3.

de Lauretis, Teresa. "The Technology of Gender." *Technologies of Gender: Essays on Theory, Film and Fiction.* Bloomington: Indiana UP, 1987. 1-30.

Deutsch, Sandra. "Gender and Sociopolitical Change in Twentieth-Century Latin America." *Hispanic American Historical Review* 2 (1991): 259-306.

Diamond, Elin. "Mimesis in Syncopated Time: Reading Adrienne Kennedy." *Intersecting Boundaries: The Theater of Adrienne Kennedy.* Ed. Paul Bryant-Jackson and Lois More Overbeck. Minneapolis: U of Minnesota P, 1992. 131-41.

Diccionario Pequeño Larousse Ilustrado. Ed. Ramón García-Pelayo y Gross. Mexico: Larousse, 1986.

Dirlik, Arif. "Culturism as Hegemonic Ideology and Liberating Practices." *Cultural Critique* 6 (1987): 13-50.

———. "The Postcolonial Aura: Third World Criticism in the Age of Global Capitalism." *Critical Inquiry* 20 (1994): 328-56.

Dolan, Jill. *The Feminist Spectator as Critic.* Ann Arbor: University Microfilms, 1988.

Eidelberg, Teresa. "Susana Torres Molina, destacada teatrista argentina." *Alba de América: Revista Literaria* 7 (1989): 391-93.

Esquivel, Laura. *Como agua para chocolate.* Barcelona: Mondadori, 1994.

Fagundes Telles, Lygia. *A Disciplina do Amor: Fragmentos.* Rio de Janeiro: Editora Nova Fronteira, 1980.

Fernandes, Nancy, and Maria Theresa Vargas. *Uma atriz: Cacilda Becker.* São Paulo: Editora Perspectiva, 1983.

Flores, Bettina, R. *Chiquita's Cocoon.* Granite Bay: Pepper Vine Press, 1990.

Fornes, Maria Irene. *Fefu and Her Friends.* New York: Paj, 1978.

Foster, David William. *Cultural Diversity in Latin America.* Albuquerque: U of New Mexico P, 1994.

———. *Gay and Lesbian Themes in Latin American Writing.* Austin: U of Texas P, 1991.

———. "Identidades polimórficas y planteo metateatral en *Extraño juguete* de Susana Torres Molina." *Alba de América: Revista Literaria* 7 (1989): 75-86.

———. "The Manipulation of the Horizons of Reader Expectations in Two Examples of Argentine Lesbian Writing: Discourse Power and Alternative Sexuality." Spanish and Portuguese Distinguished Lecture Series. Boulder: U of Colorado, 1989.

France, Anna Kay and P. J. Corso, eds. *International Women Playwrights: Voices of Identity and Transformation.* Proceedings of the First International Conference, October 18-23, 1988. Matuchen: Scarecrow, 1993.

Franco, Jean. "A Touch of Evil: Jesusa Rodríguez's Subversive Church." *The Drama Review* 17 (1992): 48-61.

———. "Going Public: Rehabiting the Private." *On Edge: The Crisis of Contemporary Latin American Culture.* Ed. George Yúdice, Jean Franco, and Juan Flores. Minneapolis: U of Minnesota P, 1992. 65-84.

———. *Plotting Women. Gender and Representation in Mexico.* New York: Columbia UP, 1989.

———. "Self-Destructing Heroines." *Minnesota Review* 22 (1984): 105-15.

Gambaro, Griselda. "¿Es posible y deseable una dramaturgia específicamente femenina?" *Latin American Theatre Review* 13.2 (1980): 17-22.

———. "Interview." *Interviews with Contemporary Women Playwrights.* Ed. Kathleen Betsko and Rachel Koening. New York: Beech Tree Books, 1987. 184-99.

Garber, Marjorie. *Vested Interests: Cross-dressing and Cultural Anxiety.* New York: Harper Collins, 1993.

Gibson, Charles. *Spain in America.* New York: Harper and Row, 1966.

Gibson, Claire. *Signs and Symbols.* New York: Saraband, 1996.

Gilbert, Sandra M., and Susan Gubar. "Masterpiece Theatre: An Academic Melodrama." *Critical Inquiry* 17 (1991): 694-717.

Gómez de Avellaneda, Gertrudis. *Sab.* Havana: Editorial Arte y Literature, 1976.

Graham-Jones, Jean. "Myth, Masks, and Machismo: Un trabajo fabuloso by Ricardo Halac and . . . *Y a otra cosa mariposa* by Susana Torres Molina." *Gestos* 10.20 (1995): 91-106

Gutierrez, Felix and Jorge Reina Schement. "Spanish International Network: The Flow of Television from Mexico to the United States." *Communication Research* 11 (1984): 241-59.

Guzik, Alberto. "Elas jogam o jogo do tempo." *O Estado de São Paulo* September 9, 1986: 8A.

———. "A mulher no palco." *O Estado de São Paulo* November 10, 1985: 10A.

Hamermesh, Mira. *Maids and Madams.* Documentary. Filmakers Library Anti-Apartheid Collection. New York, NY. Library.

Hart, Lynn, ed. *Making a Spectacle: Feminist Essays on Contemporary Women's Theatre.* Ann Arbor: U of Michigan P, 1989.

Hartmann, Heidi. "The Family as the Locus of Gender, Class, and Political Struggle: The Example of Housework." *Signs* 6 (1981): 336-94.

Helena, Lúcia. "A personagem femenino na ficção brasileiranos anos 70 e 80: Problemas teóricos é históricos." *Luso-Brazilian Review* 26.2 (1989): 43-57.

Hessel, Lothar, and Georges Readers. *O teatro no Brasil sob Dom Pedro II.* Porto Alegre: Editora da Universidade de Rio Grande de Sul, 1986.

hooks, bell. *Feminist Theory from Margin to Center.* Boston: South End Press, 1984.

———. *Talking Back: Thinking Feminist, Thinking Black.* Boston: South End Press, 1989.

Houston, Velina H. Introduction. *The Politics of Life: Four Plays by Asian American Women.* Ed. Houston. Philadelphia: Temple UP, 1993. 1-32.

———. *Tea.* Unpublished Script.

Jameson, Fredric. Afterword. *Aesthetics and Politics.* By Theodor Adorno, Walter Benjamin, Ernst Bloch, Bertolt Brecht, and Georg Lukács. London: Verso, 1986. 4-21.

Jenkins, Linda W. "Feminist Theatre." *Women in American Theatre.* Ed. Helen Krich Chinoy and Linda W. Jenkins. New York: Crown, 1981. 274-75.

Kaminsky, Amy. "Issues for an International Feminist Literary Criticism." *Signs* 19 (1993): 213-27.

———. *Reading the Body Politic: Feminist Criticism of Latin American Women Writers.* Minneapolis: U of Minnesota P, 1993.

Kanellos, Nicolás. *A History of Hispanic Theater in the United States: Origins to 1940.* Austin: U of Texas P, 1990.

Kennedy, Adrienne. *A Movie Star Has to Star in Black and White. In One Act.* Minneapolis: U of Minnesota P, 1988. 79-103.

———. *The Owl Answers. In One Act.* Minneapolis: U of Minnesota P, 1988. 25-45.

Kirkpatrick, Gwen. "The Journalism of Alfonsina Storni: A New Approach to Women's History in Argentina." *Women, Culture and Politics in Latin America.* Ed. Emilie Bergmann. Berkeley: U of California P, 1990. 105-29.

Kronik, John W. "Editor's Column." *PMLA* 106 (1991): 1034-35.

Laforgue, Jorge, ed. *El teatro argentino.* Buenos Aires: Centro Editor de América Latina, 1982.

Lamont, Rosette C. "Book Review." *Modern Drama* 32 (1989): 159-61.

Larson, Catherine. "Playwrights of Passage: Women and Game Playing on the Stage." *Latin American Literary Review* 19 (1991): 77-89.

Lope de Vega, Félix. *El arte nuevo de hacer comedias.* Mexico: Fondo de Cultura Económica, 1977.

López, Ana. "The Melodrama in Latin America." *Wide Angle* 7 (1985): 5-13.

López, Josefina. *Confessions of Women From East L.A.* Woodstock: Dramatic Publishing, 1997.

———. *Food for the Dead and La Piñata.* Woodstock: Dramatic Publising, 1997.

———. "On Being a Playwright." *Ollantay* 2 (1993): 43-46.

———. *Real Women Have Curves.* Seattle: Rain City Projects, 1988.

———. *Simply María or The American Dream. Shattering the Myth: Plays by Hispanic Women.* Ed. Linda Feyder. Houston: Arte Público, 1992. 113-41.

———. *Unconquered Spirits.* Woodstock: Dramatic Publishing, 1997.

López-Gónzalez, Aralia, Amelia Malagamba, and Elena Urrutia, eds. *Mujer y literatura mexicana y chicana.* Tijuana, B. C. : El Colegio de la Frontera Norte, 1988.

Magaldi, Sábato. *Prefácio. Da fala ao grito.* Ed. Moysés Baumstein. São Paulo: Edições Símbolo, 1977. 11-19.

Martín, Luis. *Daughters of the Conquistadores: Women of the Viceroyalty of Peru.* Albuquerque: U of New Mexico P, 1983.

Marranca, Bonnie and Gautam Dasgupta, eds. *Interculturalism and Performance.* New York: Paj, 1991.

Mastretta, Angeles. *Arráncame la vida.* Mexico: Cal y Arena, 1989.

Maufort, Marc. Ed. *Staging Difference: Cultural Pluralism in American Theatre and Drama.* New York, Peter Lang, 1995.

McClintock, Anne. "The Angel of Progress: Pitfalls of the Term 'Postcolonialism.'" *Social Text* 31 (1992): 84-98.

Mertes, Cara. "There's No Place Like Home: Women and Domestic Labor." *Dirt and Domesticity: Constructions of the Feminine.*

Ed. Jesús Fuenmayor, Kate Haug, and Frazer Ward. New York: Whitney Museum of American Art, 1992. 58-73.

Michalski, Yan. *O palco amordaçado.* Rio de Janeiro: Avenir Editora, 1979.

———. *O teatro sob pressão: uma frente de resistência.* Rio de Janeiro: Jorge Zahar, 1985.

Mignolo, Walter D. "Colonial and Postcolonial Discourse: Cultural Critique or Academic Colonialism." *Latin American Research Review* 3 (1993): 120-31.

Milleret, Margo. "Entrapment and Flight of Fantasy in Three Plays be Leilah Assunção." *Luso-Brazilian Review* 21.1 (1984): 49-56.

Millet, Kate. *Sexual Politics.* 1970. London: Virago, 1977.

Mistral, Gabriela. *Selected Poems of Gabriela Mistral.* Trans. and ed. Doris Dana. Baltimore: Johns Hopkins UP, 1971. 214-15.

Mohanty, Chandra T. "Cartographies of Struggle: Third World Women and the Politics of Feminism." *Third World Women and the Politics of Feminism.* Ed. Chandra T. Mohanty, Ann Russo, and Lourdes Torres. Bloomington: Indiana UP, 1992. 1-47.

Mohr, Nicholasa. "Puerto Rican Writers in the U.S., Puerto Rican Writers in Puerto Rico: A Separation beyond Language." *Breaking Boundaries: Latina Writing and Critical Readings.* Ed. Asunción Horno-Delgado, Eliana Ortega, Nina M. Scott, and Nancy Saporta Sternback. Amherst: U of Massachusetts P, 1989. 111-16.

Moraga, Cherríe. "For an Art of Resistance." *Crossroads* 31 (1993): 2-5.

Mulvey, Laura. "Film and Visual Pleasure." *Film Theory and Criticism.* Ed. Gerald Mast and Marshall Cohen. Oxford: Oxford UP, 1985. 803-16.

Munich, Adrianne. "Notorious Signs: Feminist Criticism and Literary Tradition." *Making a Difference: Feminist Literary Criticism.* Ed. Gayle Green and Coppélia Kahn. New York: Routledge, 1988. 238-57.

Murray, Timothy. *Like a Film: Ideological Fantansy on Screen, Camara and Canvas.* London: Routledge, 1993.

Nigro, Kirsten. "Fractured Narratives in Mexican Theater." *Negotiating Performance, Gender, Sexuality, and Theatricality in Latin/o America.* Ed. Juan Villegas and Diana Taylor. Durham: Duke UP, 1994. 137-58.

Noriega, Chon. "Between a Weapon and a Formula: Chicano Cinema and Its Contexts." *Chicanos and Film: Representation and Resistance.* Minneapolis: U of Minnesota P, 1992. 141-67.

Nuiry, Octavio E. "The Hollywood-Washington Connection." *Hispanic* Oct. 1993: 14-22.

Ordaz, Luis. *Breve historia del teatro argentino.* Buenos Aires: Editorial Universitaria, 1962.

Palmer, Phyllis. *Domesticity and Dirt: Housewives and Domestic Servants in the United States, 1920-1945.* Philadelphia: Temple UP, 1989.

Peixoto, Fernando. *Teatro em movimento (1959-1984).* São Paulo: Hucitec, 1985.

———. *Teatro em pedaços (1959-1977).* São Paulo: Hucitec, 1980.

Perkins, Kathy A. and Roberta Uno, eds. *Contemporary Plays by Women of Color.* London: Routledge, 1996.

Poniatowska, Elena. *Hasta no verte, Jesús mío.* Mexico: Ediciones Era, 1984.

———. "Puente de Ida y Vuelta." *La Jornada Semanal* 2 June 1989: 2-5.

Portillo Trambley, Estela. *Sor Juana. Sor Juana and Other Plays.* Tempe, Arizona: Bilingual Press/Editorial Bilingüe, 1983. 143-89.

Prida, Dolores. *Coser y Cantar: A Bilingual Fantasy For Two Women. Beautiful Señoritas and Other Plays.* Houston: Arte Público Press, 1991. 47-67.

———. "The Show Does Go On (testimonio)." *Breaking Boundaries. Latina Writing and Critical Readings.* Ed. Asunción Horno Delgado, Eliana Ortega, Nina M. Scott, and Nancy Saporta Sternbach. Amherst: U of Massachusetts P, 1989. 181-88.

Reinelt, Janelle, Ed. *Crucibles of Crisis: Performing Social Change.* Ann Arbor; Michigan UP, 1996.

Ribeiro, Maria Angélica. *O Teatro no Brasil: Sob Dom Pedro II.* Ed. Lothar Hessel and Georges Readers. Porto Alegre: Universidade do Rio Grande do Sul, 1986.

Richard, Nelly. "Diálogos no hemisfério Ocidental: linguagem, discurso, e política." *Simpósio: Identidade Artística e Cultural da América Latina.* 24 Sep. 1991. São Paolo, Brazil.

———. *La estratificación de los márgenes.* Santiago de Chile: Francisco Zegers, 1989.

———. *Masculino/Femenino: Prácticas de la diferencia y cultura democrática.* Santiago de Chile: Francisco Zegers, 1993.

Rios, Katheryn L. "There Are no Chicanas in Maquiladoras: Difference and Identity in Context." Unpublished paper. Berkeley: University of California. Spring 1991.

Rodriguez, Richard. "Soy Indio." *Mac Neil/Lehrer News Hour.* Public Television. Washington and New York. 6 March 1994.

Rollins, Judith. *Between Women: Domestics and Their Employers.* Philadelphia: Temple UP, 1985.

Rosaldo, Renato. *Culture and Truth: The Remaking of Social Analysis.* Boston: Beacon Press, 1989.

Rouquié, Alain. *The Military and the State in Latin America.* Trans. Paul E. Sigmund. Berkeley: U of California P, 1987.

Sadlier, Darlene J. *One Hundred Years After Tomorrow: Brazilian Women's Fiction in the 20th Century.* Ed. and trans. Darlene J. Sadlier. Bloomington: Indiana UP, 1992.

Said, Edward W. *The World, the Text and the Critic.* Cambridge: Harvard UP, 1983.

Sánchez-Scott, Milcha, and Jeremy Blahnik. *Latina. Necessary Theater: Six Plays About the Chicano Experience.* Ed. Jorge Huerta. Houston: Arte Público, 1989. 85-141.

———. *Roosters. On New Ground.* New York: Theatre Communications Group, 1987. 243-80.

Sandoval, Alberto. "Dolores Prida's *Coser y cantar:* Mapping the Dialectics of Ethnic Identity and Assimilation." *Breaking Boundaries. Latina Writing and Critical Readings.* Ed. Asunción Horno-Delgado, Eliana Ortega, Nina M. Scott, and Nancy Saporta Sternbach. Amherst: U of Massachusetts P, 1989. 201-19.

Schaller, Susy So. "Forget Me Not America." *Poster.* Seattle: The Amerasian Network, 1988.

Schroeder, Patricia R. *The Feminist Possibilities of Dramatic Realism.* Madison: Fairleigh Dickson, 1996.

Segura, Denise A. "Chicanas and Immigrant Women in the Labor Market: A Study of Occupational Mobility and Stratification." Diss. U of California, Berkeley, 1986.

Shange, Ntozake. *for colored girls who have considered suicide when the rainbow is enuf.* New York: Bantam Books, 1976.

Shohat, Ella. "Notes on the Postcolonial." *Social Text* 31/32 (1992): 99-153.

Singh, Yvonne. *Staging in the Funnyhouse: The Dramaturgy of Adrienne Kennedy.* Diss. Cornell University, 1998.

Steel, Cynthia. "The Other Within: Class and Ethnicity as Difference in Mexican Women's Literature." *Cultural and Historical Groundings for Hispanic and Luso-Brazilian Feminist Literary Criticism.* Ed. Hernán Vidal. Minneapolis: Institute for the Study of Ideologies and Literature, 1989. 297-328.

Stephens, Thomas M. *Dictionary of Latin American Racial and Ethnic Terminology.* Gainesville: U of Florida P, 1989.

Stimpson, Catharine R. "Ad/d Feminan: Women, Literature, and Society." *Literature and Society.* Ed. Edward W. Said. Baltimore: Johns Hopkins UP, 1980. 174-92.

Szoka, Elzbieta, and Joe W. Bratcher, III, eds. *3 Contemporary Brazilian Plays.* Austin: Host Publications, 1988.

Takaki, Ronald. *A Different Mirror: A History of Multicultural America.* Boston: Little, Brown, 1993.

———. *Iron Cages: Race and Culture in Nineteenth Century America.* New York: Knopf, Random House, 1979.

Taylor, Diana. *Theatre of Crisis: Drama and Politics in Latin America.* Lexington: UP of Kentucky, 1991.

———. and Juan Villegas, eds. *Negotiating Performance: Gender, Sexuality, and Theatricality in Latin/o America.* Durham: Duke UP, 1996.

Torres Molina, Susana. *Amantísima.* Unpublished manuscript.

———. *Canto de sirenas.* Unpublished manuscript.

———. *Dueña y señora.* Buenos Aries: Ediciones la Campana, 1983.

———. *Espiral de fuego.* Unpublished manuscript.

———. *Extraño juguete.* Buenos Aires: Editorial Apex, 1978.

———. *Impresiones de una futura mamá. Dueña y señora.* Buenos Aires: Ediciones la Campana, 1983. 83-93.

———. *Inventario.* Unpublished manuscript.

———. *Manifiesto.* Unpublished manuscript.

———. *Soles.* Unpublished manuscript.

———. *Unión mística.* Private publication.

Turner, Doris J. "Black Theater in a Racial Democracy: The Case of Brazilian Experimental Theater." *College Language Association Journal* 30 (1986): 30-45.

Valenzuela, Luisa. "Mis brujas favoritas." *Theory and Practice of Feminist Literary Criticism.* Ed. Gabriela Mora and Karen S. Van Hooft. Ypsilanti, Michigan: Bilingual Press, 1982. 88-95.

Vidal, Hernán. "The Concept of Colonial and Postcolonial Discourse." *Latin American Research Review* 3 (1993): 113-19.

Villegas, Juan. *Ideología y discurso crítico sobre el teatro de España y América Latina.* Minneapolis: Prism Institute, 1988.

Viramontes, Helena María. Nopalitos: The Making of Fiction. *Making Face, Making Soul. Haciendo Caras: Creative and Critical Perspectives by Women of Color.* Ed. Gloria Anzaldúa. San Francisco: Aunt Lute, 1990. 291-94.

———. Unpublished reading. 11 April 1991. Ithaca, NY: Cornell University.

Vitale, Ida. "Interview." *Historias íntimas: conversaciones con diez escritoras latinoamericanas.* Ed. and interv. Magdalena García-Pinto. Hanover: Ediciones del Norte, 1988. 253-81.

Ward, Frazer. *Preface. Dirt and Domesticity: Constructions of the Feminine.* New York: Whitney Museum, 1992. 6-7.

Warhol, Robyn R., and Diane Price Herndl, eds. *Feminisms: An Anthology of Literary Theory and Criticism.* New Brunswick: Rutgers UP, 1991.

Wehling, Susan Rita. *Feminist Discourse in Latin American Women Playwrights.* Diss. U of Cincinnati, 1992.

Wilentz, Gay. *Binding Cultures: African and African-American Women Writers.* Bloomington: Indiana UP, 1992.

Williams, Patricia. *The Alchemy of Race and Rights: Diary of a Law Professor.* Cambridge: Harvard UP, 1992.

Winn, Steven. "Protest Theater Alive in the Mission." *San Francisco Chronicle* April 21, 1992: E1-E3.

Witte, Ann. "Feminismo e anti-feminismo em Leilah Assunção e Millôr Fernandes." *Dactylus* 9 (1989): 15-20.

Wolf, Naomi. *The Beauty Myth: How Images of Female Beauty Are Used Against Women.* New York: W. Morrow, 1991.

Woolf, Virginia. *A Room of One's Own.* New York: Harcourt, Brace and World, 1929.

Yarbro-Bejaramo, Yvonne. "The Female Subject in Chicano Theatre: Sexuality, 'Race,' and Class." *Performing Feminisms: Feminist Critical Theory and Theatre.* Ed. Sue-Ellen Case. Baltimore: Johns Hopkins UP, 1990. 131-49.

Ybarra-Fausto, Tomás. "The Chicano Movement in a Multicultural/Multinational Society." *On Edge: The Crisis of Contemporary Latin AmericanCulture.* Ed. George Yúdice, Jean Franco, and Juan Flores. Minneapolis: U of Minnesota P, 1992. 207-15.

Zanato, Ilka Marinho. "A arte de quatro mulheres nos palcos do Rio." *O Estado de São Paulo* 27 March 1983: 34.

INDEX

A

Alba y las once mil vírgenes, 71,
Amaral, Maria Adelaide, 23, 27,
American minorities, 73,
Americanized social behavior, 7,
Americas, 1, 4, 10, 16-18, 57, 95, 97,
A mulher no teatro brasileiro, 22, 25,
Arte nuevo de hacer comedias, 13,
Aristotelian Theater, 63-64,
Assunção, Leilah, 18, 23, 25, 27,
Avellaneda, Gertrudis Gómez de, 12, 41,
Aviso prévio, 25,

B

Barrios, Domitila, 8,
Beauvoir, Simone de, 3, 28,
Becker, Cacilda, 23,
Behn, Aphra, 4, 57,
Berman, Sabina, 2, 58-62,
Bosi, Alfredo, 21,
Boullosa, Carmen, 18-19, 44-45, 55, 58-70, 96,
Brechtian format, 19, 74,
Brownmiller, Susan, 2,

Butler, Judith, 2-3, 86-87,

C

Calderón de la Barca, 20,
Câmara, Isabel, 23, 26,
Case, Sue-Ellen, 4, 6, 71,
Castellanos, Rosario, 57-59,
Castro, Consuelo de, 24-27,
Catholic Church, 61, 82-83,
Chicanas, 1-2, 6-9, 39, 60,
Chicanized, 19,
Chicano film, 79,
Chicano theater, 9, 74, 79, 89,
Christian missionaries, 21, 41,
Cixous, Hélène, 3, 64,
Clara, Maria, 22,
Class-centered analysis, 5,
Cocinar hombres, 18-19, 63-71, 95-96,
Como agua para chocolate, 69,
Constructions of gender, 21,
Constructions of "race", 21,
Coser y cantar, 78,
"Cross-dressing", 47, 50, 52,
"Cultural constructions", 33,
Culturalism as Hegemonic Ideology and Liberating Practice, 16,

D

Days of Obligation:

Conversations with my Mexican Father, 60,
Desire, 18-19, 46-55, 63-69, 81, 85, 95-97,
Diamond, Elin, 9-10,
"Difference", 8, 19-20, 31, 33, 71, 73-92, 95-96,
Dirlik, Arif, 16,
Dirt, 30-33,
Domestic Sphere, 11-13, 27-39,
Domesticity, 12-13, 27-39, 69,
Dramatic bodies, 57-69,
Dramatic space, 54, 64, 75,
Dramatic time, 19, 30, 63, 95,
Dupla jornada de trabalho, 18, 39-40,
Dew, C.L. Barney, 5,

E

Écriture féminine 63-64, 71,,
El eterno femenino, 59, 62, 67,
El gran teatro del mundo, 20,
El Hábito, 54, 62,
El suplicio del placer, 2,
Empregada doméstica, 34,
Esquivel, Laura, 61, 69,
Experimental theater, 18, 44-46, 90,

F

Fefu and Her Friends, 90,
Feminine dramaturgy, 19, 62-63, 71, 95,
Femininity, 2,
Feminisms, 1-6, 18, 41-42, 57, 95-97,
Feminist ideology, 19, 43, 58, 63, 95,
Feminist literary criticism, 1-4,
for colored girls who have considered suicide when the rainbow is enuf, 77,
Forget Me Not America, 88-89,
Fornes, Maria Irene, 90,
Franco, Jean, 11, 59-61,
Fuentes, 21,

G

Gainor, Ellen, 4,
Gambaro, Griselda, 3, 13, 42-43, 49, 55,
Gandersheim, Hrotsvit von, 4,
Garber, Margorie, 45, 50, 52-53,
Gender, 1-3, 9, 17, 25-32, 45-47, 62-71, 75-93, 96-97,
Gender act theory, 2-3,
Gender categories, 3, 19, 46, 51, 55, 96,
Gendered self, 2, 29,
Gender system, 2,
Genre, 1, 16, 21-23, 59, 75, 92,
Gestos, 9,
Glantz, Margo, 62,
Gonzaga, Chiquinha, 22,

H

Happily Ever After, 81-82,
Hart, Lynn, 12,

Hasta no verte Jesús mío, 60,
Herndl, Diane Price, 3, 5,
Hessel, Lothar, 22,
Heterosexuality, 5, 18-19, 46, 51-55, 67, 96-97,
Hill, Rosana, 27,
Hilst, Hilda, 23,
Hispanic, 1, 13, 57-58, 74, 76, 90,
História concisa da literatura brasileira, 21,
Holy Trinity, 83,
Homoeroticism, 41, 45, 51-55,
Homosexuality, 19, 27, 46-55, 67, 96,
hooks, bell, 9-10, 88,
Houston, Velina Hasu, 9, 76-77, 86,

I

Ideal woman, 2,
Indigenous populations, 8, 10-11, 41, 60,
Internalized racism, 36, 77,

J

K

Kanellos, Nicolás, 74,
Kaplan, Cora, 5,
Kirkpatrick, Gwen, 14,
Kusnet, Eugênio, 27,

L

La Adelita, 11,
Lampião, 21,
Las Comadres, 75,
Latina, 18, 58, 68, 78-79, 84-94, 96-97,
Lauter, Paul, 5,
Law, Carolyn, 5,
Leite, Luiza Barreto, 22,
Lesbian feminism and theater, 4,
Lesbians, 27,
Limpieza de sangre, 10,
Linha dura, 24,
López, Josefina, 2, 18, 39, 49, 59-60, 85, 88-90, 97,
Lua nua, 18, 29-30, 35-40, 92, 96,

M

Machismo, 16,
Maestras, 14,
Maids, 39, 86, 91,
Man (biological category), 2,
Maquiladora industries, 7,
Marginal actors, 17, 20, 77,
Maria de Jesus, Carolina, 8,
Materialist feminist perspective, 5, 33-37, 71-72, 96,
Materialist methodology, 1, 71, 96,
Menchú, Rigoberta, 8,
Mestizo, 8, 11, 60,
Mexican Revolution, 11,

Mexico, 1, 7, 57-71, 80, 88-91,
Michalski, Yan, 24, 38-39,
Millet, Kate, 4,
Misogynist ideology, 1, 48-51,
Mistral, Gabriela, 14,
Mohanty, Chandra, 6,
Molina, Susana Torres, 3, 18, 42-55, 63, 96,
Mohr, Nicholasa, 8,
Moraga, Cherríe, 9, 74, 76, 88, 90,
Motherhood, 14, 18, 35, 43, 67-68,

N

North American suffragist plays, 1930s-40s, 4,
Nuyorican, 8,

O

O Estado de São Paulo, 22, 25,
O palco amordaçado, 24, 27,
Os Cancros Socias, 12,
Os Comediantes, 22,
O teatro no Brasil sob Dom Pedro II, 22,

P

Pallottini, Renata, 23, 27,
Pan-American feminist political organizations, 14,
Patriarchal chavinism, 49, 61-69, 97,

Patrõa, 32, 36,
Performances of power, 3, 6, 20,
Performing border identities, 73-78,
Phallocentrism, 1, 50,
Poniatowska, Elena, 8-9, 12, 60,
Popular culture, 19, 49, 79-82, 91,
Popular narratives, 79, 89, 92,
Portillo-Trambley, Estela, 58, 76,
Prida, Dolores, 76, 78, 91,
Private sphere, 18, 97,
Propusieron a María, 71,
Public sphere, 11, 29-31, 37-38
Puerto Rican Writers in the U.S., Puerto Rican Writers in Puerto Rico: A Separation beyond Language, 8,

Q

Queiroz, Rachel de, 21,

R

Race (cultural construct), 1, 12, 27-37, 60, 71, 88, 95-96,
Racial superiority, 36, 49,
Radical feminist lesbian position, 4, 41, 58,
Radical women's theater, 4, 41, 51, 58,
Readers, Georges, 22,
Real Women Have Curves, 2,

Realism, 91,
Respuesta a Sor Filotea, 57,
Ribeiro, Maria Angélica, 11-12, 22, 41, 97,
Rodríguez, Jesusa, 54, 61-62,
Rodriguez, Richard, 60-63,
Rollins, Judith, 37,
Rouquié, Alain, 14,

S

Sab 12,,
Said, Edward, 16,
Sainetes, 41,
Sánchez-Scott, Milcha, 68, 85, 91,
Schaller, Susy So, 88,
Segall, Lasar, 26,
Sexual Politics, 4,
Shange, Ntozake, 9, 77, 90,
Simply María or the American Dream, 18-19, 59, 71, 78-92,
Soap operas, 79, 81, 91,
Soldaderas, 11,
Sor Juana Inés de la Cruz, 4, 12, 57-59, 97,
Singh, Yvonne, 10,
S.O.S. é uma lésbica, 27,
Spanish comedies, 41,
Spanish Renaissance society, 13,
Staging in the Funnyhouse: The Dramaturgy of Adrianne Kennedy, 10, 77,
Storni, Alfonsina, 14, 41,

T

Tangos, 19, 49-50,
Teatro experimental do Negro, 37-39,
Teatro herético, 63, 71,
Telenovelas, 81-82,
Theatre of Crisis: Drama and Politics in Latin America, 15,
The Journalism of Alfonsina Storni: A New Approach to Women's History in Argentina, 14,
The Latin American Theatre Review, 9, 25,
The Military and the State in Latin America, 14,
There are no Chicanas in Maquiladoras: Difference and Identity in Context, 7,
The Second Sex, 3, 28,
Third-world women, 6-7,
Torres-Molina, Susana, 63, 96,
Toscano, Moema, 34,
Transvestism, 50-52, 55,
Transvestite, 18, 46, 50, 51, 96,
Trouble in Mind, 76-77,

U

Um teatro da mulher: dramaturgia feminina no palco brasileiro contemporâneo, 27, 39,

Universidade de São Paulo, 21, 25-27,
Urrutia, Elena, 60,
U.S. playwrights of color, 9, 76-91, 96,

V

Valdez, Luis, 79,
Valenzuela, Luisa, 3, 63, 66, 69,
Varga, Llosa, 21,
Vega, Lope de, 13,
Vincenzo, Elza Cunha de, 27, 39,
Villalta, Maruxa, 58,
Villegas, Juan, 16,
Viramontes, Helena María, 9,
Vitale, Ida, 16,

W

Warhol, Robyn, 3, 5,
Whiter, 9,
Witches, 55, 63-70,
Wolf, Naomi, 31,
Woman (biological category), 2, 95-96,
Woman-centered, 5,
Woman-identified heterosexual, 5,
Women, 13, 21-31, 39-40, 41-51, 57-70, 75-92, 95-97,
Women, Culture and Politics in Latin America, 14,
Women of color, 6-9, 19, 23, 36, 38-39, 60, 76-92, 96-97,

Women of the Americas, 17,
Women playwrights, 1-4, 10, 18, 21-26, 41-43, 57, 76-78, 84-90, 95,
Women's dramaturgy, 1, 76, 95,
Woolf, Virgina, 57,

X

Y

... Y a otra cosa mariposa, 3, 18, 44-54, 96,

Z

Zoot Suit, 75,

WOR(L)DS OF CHANGE
Latin American & Iberian Literature

Kathleen March, Editor

This series deals with the relationship between literary creation and the social, political, and historical contexts in which it is produced. The types of volumes may include critical analyses of one or more works by one or several authors; critical editions of important works that may have been out of print for a long time, but which represent a major contribution to literature of the Iberian Peninsula or Latin America; English translations of important works, with critical introduction. Topics for Latin America include: studies of representative works of nineteenth- and twentieth-century thought; poetic portrayals of history; subgenres (fictionalization of the rural and urban social structures); historical novels; literature of exile; re-readings of colonial texts; new approaches to the figure of the Indian and other representatives of transculturation; women writers and other less studied authors. Topics for Spain and Portugal include: writing and nationalism in the Spanish State; bilingualism and the literary texts; censorship and exile; new and renewed genres such as autobiography and testimony; the formation of the avant-garde. Formal studies are expected to bear out the general contextual focus of the series. The use of recent developments in literary criticism is especially appropriate. The series also seeks to contribute to the understanding and accuracy of interpretation of the writing which has combined European elements with indigenous and African ones as well as to the understanding of the dynamics behind such major cultural issues as the formation of literary trends or subgenres, national identities, the effects of postcolonial status on literary imagination, the appearance and experience of women writers, and the relationships between postmodernism and Ibero American writing. The series title is inclusive of literatures that are geographically, historically, or politically related and whose comparison is relevant to Spanish and Spanish American writing. This means those written in the other three languages of Spain, in Portugal, and in Brazil. Comparative studies in which colonial or postcolonial themes are prevalent may also be appropriate, if one of the literatures is in either Spanish or Portuguese. The breadth of the geographical area is intended to provide a forum for revealing and interpreting its multicultural aspects.

For additional information about this series or for the submission of manuscripts, please contact Peter Lang Publishing, Inc., Acquisitions Department, 516 N. Charles St., 2nd Floor, Baltimore, MD 21201.

To order other books in this series, please contact our Customer Service Department at: (800) 770-LANG (within the U.S.), (212) 647-7706 (outside the U.S.), (212) 647-7707 FAX, or browse online by series at: www.peterlang.com.